The Magnificent Gift
of
Agency

The Magnificent Gift
of
Agency

To Act and Not Be Acted Upon

Gary C. Lawrence

Author of
How Americans View Mormonism
Mormons Believe ... What?!
The War in Heaven Continues

© 2020

Published by
Parameter Publishing, LLC
Santa Ana, CA

office@parameterpublishing.com

ISBN-13   978-0-9906342-2-5

Cover design, editing, and layout by Stephanie Smith
Cover image: amasterphotographer/Shutterstock.com

Printed in the United States of America

In appreciation for those who
care enough about agency to defend it.

"The preservation of agency is more important
than the preservation of life itself."
— Marion G. Romney

Contents

Preface

"Agents or objects?" That is the question.

As a public opinion researcher, I have measured increasing polarization in recent years. Where I previously saw bell-shaped curves while mapping attitudes on a continuum, I now see U-shaped curves. On issue after issue, people are gravitating toward distinct and opposite points of view, often intensely so. Fewer remain in the middle.

The more I analyzed increasing divisions in society, the more apparent became the role of agency – a matter of acting or being acted upon as society's squabbles pushed people to choose where they will stand.

So I decided to write a book about it and the premise came clear:

> **Every human behavior and every event in history can be more accurately explained by the adherence to or violation of agency than by any other explanation.**

Being agents unto ourselves, we have the natural right to run our own lives and call our own shots. Those who honor and actively apply agency enjoy blessings of creativity, prosperity, refinement, and progress. Those who dwindle in appreciation for it become objects – puppets on strings – and reap the stale life of robots.

Beyond exploring agency in numerous applications, I especially wrote this book to warn against those who seek to exercise unrighteous dominion and restrict our agency by acting upon us in devious ways.

I hope it will encourage us to vigorously defend God's magnificent gift against them.

As social mores change and attitudes intensify, the world will indeed divide into two camps and man's agency will play an even more important role. How we use this great power to act and not be acted upon is up to us.

Will we be agents or objects?

Gary C. Lawrence
Orange County, California
Spring, 2020

Introduction

The Gift

"Next to the bestowal of life itself, the right
to direct that life is God's greatest gift to man."
– David O. McKay

Agency is the freedom to think and choose;
the power to act; to experience and learn from the
consequences; and to be responsible and accountable.

The Father desires we use this gift to become as He is.

Agency is impossible without
the Savior's Atonement.

With the freedom to run our own lives,
we make mistakes.

Mistakes must have consequences
or there is no justice.

To learn from mistakes,
we must have the opportunity to
try again or we will never progress.

Agency therefore requires
both justice and mercy.

With sincere repentance,
the Atonement releases us from
the punishments of justice.

Agency thrives.

Ask the average person to define *agency* and he will typically refer to an organization such as an employment, talent, or government agency.

Ask that person to describe *agent* and you may hear about the FBI, CIA spies, or free agents in the National Football League.

Those who come closest to how God uses the word are those who have hired someone who acts on their behalf as a representative, go-between, proxy or negotiator – as their agent.

Perhaps the agent is a lawyer hired to act on behalf of another in a legal matter. Or a financial agent to represent them in monetary matters. Or a talent agent to find them an acting gig in a movie.

In these examples, Person A hires Person B.

What God means by agency, however, is that **Person A hires ... Person A.** We "hire" ourselves to be our own agents and handle all personal actions – we become agents unto ourselves with freedom and power to act.

Self-ownership. **We are sovereign over ourselves.**

> And it is given unto them to know good from evil; wherefore they are **agents unto themselves** .... [1]*

Agency and the Savior

If you think faith without works is dead, it's nothing compared to agency without the Atonement.

President Boyd K. Packer stated it bluntly: "Had agency come to man without the Atonement, it would have been a fatal gift."[2] We

---

* Wherever a word or phrase in a scripture or quote is red, bolded, italicized, or underlined, assume it is my emphasis unless stated otherwise.

would have made mistakes with absolutely no way of being released from justice. Stuck for eternity.

Lehi taught his son Jacob the Savior's role in preserving agency:

> And the Messiah cometh in the fullness of time, that he may *redeem* the children of men from the fall. And because that they are redeemed from the fall they have become *free* forever, knowing good from evil; to act for themselves and **not be acted upon** ....[3]

And Elder David A. Bednar:

> "The greatest gift that the Father gives to us is His Son, and the gift that comes to us through the Savior's atonement is agency. **Agency is central** to the Father's plan and it is the capacity to act and learn from our own experiences. That is the very essence and purpose of being here in mortality."[4]

Because we are redeemed from the fall, agency works. The Savior's Atonement allows us to act as we choose, repent of mistakes and not be in Satan's clutches forever, which would be the case in the absence of Christ's mercy.

The All-Encompassing Gift

Agency is both **a power and a commandment**, and is a deeper, more profound principle of the gospel – complex yet simple – than we may at first appreciate.

At some point in our pre-earthly existence, we received this powerful gift and began our journey as agents by choosing to follow the Father's plan and His Son's example. How we exercise it in our earthly life will determine our progress and eventual existence. It is so germane that in some deep way, agency and actions are connected to truth and existence, as alluded in D&C 93:

All truth is independent in that sphere in which God has placed it, **to act for itself**, as all intelligence also; **otherwise there is no existence**.

"Truth is independent" and can "act for itself." Why? Because a truth in one field will never contradict a truth in another field. The phrase "as all intelligence also" indicates that all intelligence is likewise independent in that sphere in which God has placed it and can also act for itself.

Because God created us as spirit beings from something called intelligence, which has always existed, we are the "intelligence" that is independent in this earthly sphere.

This independence, without which there is no existence, of necessity undergirds all of the elements in this complex gift:

It is so all-encompassing that if honored produces joy and exaltation and if violated results in stagnation and misery.

A Perspective

Over 100 billion people have lived on the earth.[5] One calculation method suggests that over 50 billion of God's spirit children chose to follow Lucifer who promised all would return to live in heaven.

When Lucifer argued his plan counter to God's, the Father did not negotiate. Our agency was and remains non-negotiable even though God knew those who chose Lucifer could never again live in His presence.

> Agency is more than the freedom to choose. It is a commandment.

If Satan's promise of equal outcomes no matter one's behavior had been instituted, God would have lost His power and we our agency.

Our Heavenly Father paid a horrific price so we would have the magnificent gift of agency.

That's how important it is!

"God is our Father. He loves us and He wants us to have joy. He does want us to have immortality and eternal life, but He wants us to choose this course. He honors our agency."[6]

– Russell M. Nelson

Exploring Agency

Because agency touches every aspect of life, books could be written on each of the 24 chapters that follow. I can present but a few glimpses into the commandment to act and not be acted upon.

In the following pages we will explore…

- How agency's creative powers spur the growth of the mind, how comparisons lead to connections that in turn lead to innovation and humor and symphonies and beauty;

- The need for action, that no one eats until someone takes a risk, the adventure in taking calculated chances;

- Opposition in all things, that there can be no movement without friction, but at the same time hostile opposition is Satan's playground;

- How the adversary tries to destroy agency, for if agency is destroyed then justice is destroyed and God ceases to be God;

- How disrespect for the agency of others leads to pride, excessive centralization, suffocating rules, improper uses of power, and controlling tyrannies;

- How acceptance or attempted avoidance of consequences is the critical fork in the road of our existence, and how intervening between an action and a consequence is not the best way to help others;

- The fruits of agency, how to enjoy life in spite of hardships, and in the process move along the path to exaltation.

The gift of agency is the opportunity to work directly with the Father to achieve exaltation and become as He is.

ℰℬ

"Agency would have no meaning without the vital contribution of Jesus Christ. His central role began with His support of the Father's plan and His willingness to become the essential Savior under that plan."
– D. Todd Christofferson

SECTION I

To Act

Chapter 1

Freedom
The Right to Run Your Own Life

"What then is freedom?
The power to live as one wishes."
– Cicero

Know this, that every soul is free, To choose his life and what he'll be;
For this eternal truth is giv'n: That God will force no man to heav'n.

He'll call, persuade, direct aright, And bless with wisdom, love, and light,
In nameless ways be good and kind, But never force the human mind.

– Traditional Hymn

We had agency
before we came to earth.

We had the freedom to choose to follow
God and His Son ... or Lucifer.

We had the freedom to
make covenants with God.

Agency and freedom are historically
and inseparably connected.

Freedom and fear vary inversely:
As freedom increases, fear decreases.

As fear decreases, happiness increases.

As happiness increases,
the ultimate goal of God's plan for us
– a fullness of joy – is obtained.

Agency begins with freedom.

Air Force pilot and Medal of Honor winner Leo Thorsness tells of fellow pilot Mike Christian's love of freedom. Shot down within days of each other, they became prisoners in the North Vietnam POW camp known as the Hanoi Hilton.

One day Mike found the remains of a dirty handkerchief tucked into a crack in a stinky building where POWs took sponge baths. He successfully hid it from the guards and over the next weeks painstakingly cleaned it with scraps of soap to make it as white as possible. He took crumpled pieces of red-tile roof, pulverized them into powder, mixed it with rice water and made a red ink. Guards would give sick prisoners a blue pill of unknown provenance and toxicity, so Mike ground down a couple and made a blue ink with which he filled in the upper left hand corner of the white rag.

The red ink was used for stripes and, with a slice of bamboo as a needle and with thread from his blanket, Mike painstakingly sewed little pieces of white cloth onto the blue background.

> "The secret to happiness is freedom … And the secret to freedom is courage."
>
> – Thucydides

One morning before the guards were awake, he said, "Hey gang, look at this." And waved that little flag. Immediately, every man stood ramrod straight and together cited the Pledge of Allegiance. It was the ugliest of flags; it was the most beautiful of flags. Tears ran down their cheeks.

They pledged allegiance to the flag and to the republic for which that flag stands. And more emphatically the freedom it symbolizes.

A few days later, the captors conducted a surprise strip search and found Mike Christian's little flag. He was beaten mercilessly for hours. After midnight, as Thorsness tells the story, they dumped him back into their cell, his face so beaten up he couldn't see and his vocal chords so damaged he couldn't talk. It took weeks for him to regain some semblance of activity.

As soon as he could, Mike Christian started looking for … another piece of cloth.

℘

The story of another famous lover of freedom began when her grandmother was shipped to America as a slave. As a child, Araminta Ross was beaten many times by her slave-masters. She later wrote, "I grew up like a neglected weed – ignorant of liberty, having no experience of it."

> "No man can put a chain about the ankle of his fellow man without at last finding the other end fastened about his own neck."
>
> – Frederick Douglass

She escaped slavery at age 27 making use of a network known as the Underground Railroad, a train on tracks being an odd visual for what was a two-to-three-week journey totally on foot.

Achieving freedom for herself was not enough; she was determined to share it. As she put it, "I had reasoned this out in my mind, there was one of two things I had a right to, liberty or death; if I could not have one, I would have the other."

Her own freedom in jeopardy, she nonetheless returned to the slave state of Maryland 13 times between 1849 and 1860 to rescue upwards of 70 slaves and guide them to freedom in Pennsylvania, or later to safer Ontario, Canada.

14

Araminta Ross, fighter for freedom, became better known to the world as …

Harriet Tubman.[1]

∾

These two stories are of the variety commonly presented when speaking of freedom – harsh, specific, visual. But freedom is even deeper than that and threats to it more subtle. We understand it better when we ask what is its opposite. And the opposite of freedom in this broader sense is simply … control. Specifically control of you by others without your permission.

Oh, the variations: tyrants and despots in numerous forms, busybodies in bloated bureaucracies, micromanaging bosses, nagging relatives, hounding elites, central planners, harassing authoritarians who rob the fruits of your labor, runaway homeowner associations, you name it. Anyone who tells you what to do and manipulates your submission violates your freedom and your God-given gift of agency.

Bars and shackles are but superfluous manifestations.

In The Big Inning

Freedom stands as the first undergirding component of agency – a **natural, always-existing state** unless man destroys it. In his King Follett Discourse, Joseph Smith explained:

> "God himself, finding he was in the midst of spirits and glory, because he was more intelligent, saw proper to institute laws whereby the rest could have a privilege to advance like himself. … He has power to institute laws to instruct the weaker intelligences …."

The freedom to act simply existed. It was and is the natural state of things. Force came later when intelligences-made-spirits unfortunately used their freedom to act upon others.

The Prophet Joseph wrote further:

> "All men are, or ought to be free, possessing <u>unalienable rights</u>, and the high and noble qualifications of the laws of nature and of self-preservation, <u>to think, and act, and say</u> as they please, while they maintain a due respect to the rights and privileges of all other creatures, infringing upon none."[2]

Freedom is simply the right to be left alone to decide one's own life. Respect for freedom correlates with adherence to and honoring of agency, which in turn increases the likelihood of achieving exaltation.

... they became subjects to follow after their own will.[3]

Organizations Also

If we have the right to run our own lives, do we not as groups of individuals also have that same right? It's obvious. Pooling our efforts for a common good is as American as church bake sales, neighborhood watch programs, and the volunteers who fired the shots heard around the world in 1775. As the apostle Paul wrote, "... where the Spirit of the Lord is, there is liberty."[4] Inseparable for individuals and groups alike.

God established the U.S. Constitution as the foundation of the nation destined to host the Restoration and promote the gathering of Israel. However, His plans could not go forward without freedom of religion, thus its primacy as the first freedom in the First Amendment in the Bill of Rights – first among firsts.

This great Amendment says "Congress shall make no law respecting an establishment of religion, or prohibiting the **free exercise** thereof;

or abridging the **freedom of speech** ....." The re-established Church robustly supports this freedom and has never sought to curtail any other religion's exercise of it, "let them worship how, where, or what they may."[5] And we recognize the freedom to have no religion at all.

What is meant by "free exercise" has tangled a few minds over the years, but it can hardly mean a member cannot tell others his beliefs, or express an opinion based on religious values. A person doesn't have to listen, but he cannot invoke the amendment to silence the speaker.

Now come people who say religious freedom is a hide-behind for abusive patriarchy, racism, homophobic bigotry, among other juicy labels. Claiming religions are hateful, they reject freedom **of** religion and substitute freedom **from** religion. Ignoring they already have both choices, their goal is to prevent religion from having a voice in the public square – that even personal opinions based on religious values should be verboten. **They believe it is not only their right not to listen, it is their right to prevent us from speaking.** (There's a reason freedom of speech immediately follows religious freedom in that Amendment.) These activists proceed as if it's their God-given right to oppose a God-given right.

Battles about religious freedom will become more numerous and intense before the Second Coming as Satan unleashes all his devices to delay his own imitation of Custer's Last Stand.

> "No ... weapon in the arsenals of the world is so formidable as the will and moral courage of free men and women."
>
> – Ronald Reagan

Manipulations

Freedom as a word can be manipulated to our detriment depending on the word that follows it. Consider the ongoing debate about four freedoms:

> Freedom of speech

> Freedom of worship

> Freedom from want

> Freedom from fear

At first glance, what's to argue? But those advocating these freedoms know what they are doing as **they mix freedoms of and freedoms from**. Huge difference. Freedoms "of" are natural rights and do not cost anyone else a dime; we guarantee them by not restricting speech or worship. But the freedoms "from" a specific *need* are not natural rights and can cost substantial money to guarantee.

> You have the right of free speech.
>
> Others have the freedom not to listen.

Freedoms "of" are tests of our tolerance of opposite points of view. Freedoms "from" are tests of our compassion.

Charity must be voluntary and motivated by love, not force. Because not everyone is charitable, suffering can be alleviated to an extent through free-will charity, but freedom from want cannot be absolutely guaranteed without the forceful taking of resources from the uncompassionate to combine with those who willingly give.

If I do not help feed the hungry of my own free will, perhaps by joining others similarly motivated, I will be answerable to God for not being generous with His blessings to me. But if I join those who forcibly take and redistribute, I will also be answerable, this time for violating the freedom of the uncompassionate who must experience the natural consequences of a test of life before they can progress.

To repeat, we do not have a natural right in this life to be free from want or free from fear. To believe such rights should be guaranteed by government distorts the true meaning of freedom and weakens agency.

Moral Agency

Agency used to be known as "free agency." More often it is now referred to as moral agency – individual freedom. "As children of our Heavenly Father," explains Elder David A. Bednar, "we have been blessed with the gift of <u>moral</u> agency, the capacity and power of <u>independent</u> action."[6]

Agency is freedom, but it's deeper than that. One can recognize the availability of choices without revering freedom. But one cannot truly revere freedom until he has witnessed or experienced its curtailment.

Life guarantees that all will sooner or later face those who would narrow our choices or pull our strings. Such busybodies may be successful in the short run, but guarantee their own defeat in the long run.

> "Morality is inconceivable without free will."
>
> – Immanuel Kant

The more oppressive forces diminish our choices, even in simple matters, the more our willingness to fight for freedom increases, corked up as it may be. As we fight for freedom on a small stage, we appreciate the principles that check abuse of power on the large stage. Whole-hearted exercise of agency naturally leads to valiance.

The important thing to recognize is that agency is not an inert freedom, a passive gift that requires nothing from us. Rather, it is a direct commandment to use our freedom to act, do, accomplish.

Consider these scriptures:

> "A society that puts equality before freedom will get neither. A society that puts freedom before equality will get a higher degree of both."
>
> – Milton Friedman

... free according to the flesh ... **free to choose** liberty and eternal life, through the great Mediator of all men, or to choose captivity and death, according to the captivity and power of the devil ...[7]

I, the Lord God, make you free, therefore ye are **free indeed** ....[8]

... ye are **free to act** for yourselves – to choose the way of everlasting death or the way of eternal life.[9]

... whosoever perisheth, perisheth unto himself; and whosoever doeth iniquity, doeth it unto himself; for behold, ye are free; ye are permitted to **act for yourselves** ....[10]

And especially:

The Spirit of God ... is also the spirit of freedom.[11]

The bottom line is all references to freedom in the scriptures of necessity relate to agency. All component parts depend upon each other – lose one and you lose them all. Elder D. Todd Christofferson explained:

"We need the justice of God – a system of fixed and immutable laws that He Himself abides by and employs – so that we can have and exercise agency. This **justice is the foundation of our freedom to act** and is our only path to ultimate happiness."[12]

Benjamin Franklin stated it succinctly: "Freedom is not a gift bestowed upon us by other men, but a right that belongs to us by the laws of God and nature" and "Only a virtuous people are capable of freedom."

In a world of competing groups and shifting labels – conservative, liberal, Democrat, Republican, left, right, progressive, independent, tea party, moderate, green, socialist, traditionalist, neo-liberal, reformist, etc. – we can cut through the confusion if we judge proposed policies by one simple question: **Will it add to or subtract from my freedom to run my own life?**

☙

The Declaration of Independence might well be called
the Declaration of Agency.

Chapter 2

Think

Ping the Brain, You Little Neurons

"The mind is not a vessel to be filled
but a fire to be kindled."

– Plutarch

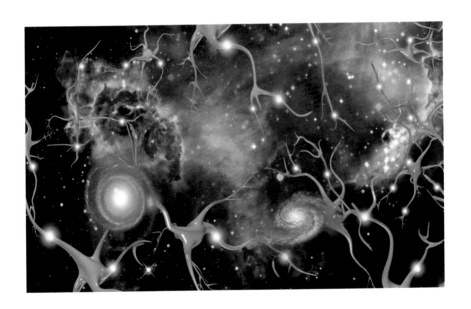

While freedom is the first *condition* of agency,
the mind is the first *instrument*.

Applied agency begins in the mind.

A stimulus from our senses
triggers mental activity.

"Hmmm, what should I do with this?"

We then search our mental networks
for related items.

We make comparisons and look for connections.

The more robust our agency,
the more choices we take time to consider.

The more choices,
the more comparisons we can make.

The more comparisons,
the greater the useful connections.

The more the connections,
the greater the insights.

Connections, insights, creativity.

The mind expands.

A 14-year-old farm boy had just plowed a potato field in Idaho and as he looked over his work at the end of the day, two seemingly unrelated visuals came together in his mind and changed history.

Thinking of the straight plowed lines, he wondered if an image could be scanned electronically as a series of lines using the same back-and-forth motions he had just used to plow the field, line by line. Thus was born the principle of the image dissector and he produced a working version at age 21 followed by the cathode ray tube that displayed the image.

The teenager who saw this connection in 1921? Philo Farnsworth, television pioneer.[1]

℃

Little Houses and Expanding Real Estate

Your brain contains 100,000,000,000 little houses and sticking out from each are one, two, three or more wires. The houses are neurons and the wires are dendrites – 'mini-computers' – each the thickness of one-hundredth the diameter of a human hair.[2]

From the stimuli of daily life, the brain picks up an item, such as Farnsworth's picture of a potato field, and using trillions of miles of dendrites sends signals to neurons asking, "Does this guy fit with you?" And if there's a possible connection, "Care to get together for a synapse?" – synapses being the gaps between dendrites across which electrical signals flow. The more frequently neurons send signals to other neurons, the more they are "glued" together to form clusters we call … thoughts.[3]

The brain constantly rewires itself. One thought triggers another – good for good, evil for evil – and less-used clusters get pruned, all based on what we choose to think about.

> "Creativity is just connecting things."
>
> – Steve Jobs

The 100 billion neuron houses in your brain are not spread out on flat real estate; they work just as well on the walls of a cliff. Because the brain is plastic and malleable, territory for new neurons and dendrites is created by digging canyons – fissures. The more fissures, the more neurons, the more the connections, the more the ideas.

This was the critical feature of the brain of a man from Ulm, Germany, who as a little boy didn't speak until he was four years old and his teachers thought was retarded, but became known as the smartest man in the world. Because of brain canyons and curiosity.

Albert Einstein – A Groovy Dude

We don't know his early mental processes, but whatever they were, they led to his brain becoming one of the most complex in history. He died in 1955 but pictures of his autopsied brain were not released until 2012. They revealed more grooves, more convolutions, more ridges and valleys, more fissures – more of that all-important surface-area gray matter – than almost any other brain ever examined.

The most striking discovery, as one report has it, was "the complexity and pattern of convolutions on certain parts of Einstein's cerebral cortex … important for the kind of abstract thinking that Einstein would have needed for his famous thought experiments on the nature of space and time. … The unusually complex pattern of convolutions there probably gave the region an <u>unusually large surface area</u>, which may have contributed to his remarkable abilities."[4]

Those grooves were formed because Einstein pushed his brain, which is what our Father, who gave us our magnificent brains, wants us to do.

Imagination

We get a hint of the power of Einstein's mental processes through the imagination scenarios he pondered – trains, the speed of light, falling painters, elevators, lightning, spaceships, flipping a two-sided coin, etc.[5] It began at age 16 when he wondered what it would be like to ride a beam of light across the universe. Then followed his famous thought experiments:

- You're standing on a train embankment watching a fast-moving train go by. At the exact time the mid-point of the train passes you, lightning strikes both ends of the train. You perceive two simultaneous lightning flashes. Would a passenger at the mid-point of that train see them as simultaneous, or does time move differently for someone who is moving?

- You have a twin who at birth is placed on a spaceship and travels through the universe at nearly the speed of light. When you're old, your twin returns to earth. Will he be as old as you or younger?

- If a man is in a free-falling elevator such that he is weightless, and he suddenly drops to the floor, is it because of gravity or because someone accelerated it by pulling upward on a rope?

- What happens if a light is shined from a train moving at the speed of light? Or, if two passengers on a train moving at the speed of light throw a ball back and forth, does the ball move faster than the speed of light when thrown in the direction the train is moving?

In the last example, if the speed of light is a constant (which it is), then either time or distance has to give way as the train speed increases. And they do. From such interplay between the neuron clusters in his brain, Einstein explained to the world that … time slows as motion increases, time and space are not absolute, gravity and acceleration are the same thing, observers in motion experience time differently, and that matter, motion, and gravity bend the fabric of the time-space continuum.[6]

His modest reaction? "I have no special talents. I am only passionately curious." Curiosity on steroids, we might argue, for he trained his brain to see complexities and similarities, and then connect them to real-world objects for the sake of us not as advanced.

> Aristotle said, "Command of metaphor is the mark of genius, for to make good metaphors implies an eye for resemblances."
>
> And as one wag put it, "Einstein never metaphor he didn't like."

Playfulness

How does it begin? With children at play:

A cardboard box becomes a car or a pirate ship. A stick becomes a horse or a flying broom. Put Cheerios in a line and you have a train. Donuts become wheels; oranges become bowling balls; chairs and blankets become a castle or a fort; with capes you can fly. (I have a relative who tried that off a garage roof – imagination takes you only so far.)

And the character swaps:

"I'm her; I get to be the queen." "No, I get to be the queen; you can be a princess." "I know, we'll both be princesses and Suzie can be queen." (Ever wonder where mankind's royalty obsessions began?)

What a great mental condition to be amenable, even prepared, for anything to happen. Playfulness is a willingness to suspend reality, to go where curiosity leads. Such a mind keeps pinging the brain for new comparisons and enjoys building on the connections and combinations that result.

Thus, everything is feasible to children. Isn't this what we would want our brain to do – check out every possibility, even though many may appear useless, even silly, at first?

Eric Hoffer noted: "The creative mind is the playful mind. When the Greeks said, 'Whom the gods love die young,' they probably meant that those favored by the gods stay young till the day they die; young and playful."

As Einstein himself put it: "To stimulate creativity, one must develop the childlike inclination for play. **Creativity is intelligence having fun.**"

Effort

The mind is a whirlwind of activity that must be channeled to be productive. Organizing and focusing it doesn't happen automatically. It takes effort. The well-known story of Oliver Cowdery is illustrative.

Oliver, serving as the Prophet Joseph's scribe, desired to have the same gift of translation and try his hand at it. The Lord humored him and as he sat there like a receptive sponge, nothing happened. Then the explanation:

Behold, you have not understood; you have supposed that I would give it unto you, when you **took no thought** save it was to ask me.

But, behold, I say unto you, that you must **study it out in your mind**; then you must ask me if it be right, and if it is right I will cause that your bosom shall burn within you; therefore, you shall feel that it is right.

But if it be not right thou shall have no such feelings, but you shall have a stupor of thought ....

Now, if you had known this you could have translated ....[7]

Harness neurons and dendrites through study and effort, such as from the best books:

And as all have not faith, seek ye diligently and teach one another words of wisdom; yea, seek ye out of the best books words of wisdom; seek learning, even by study and also by faith.[8]

Sometimes the reward trickles in a bit at a time. Other times it's sudden. On September 12, 1933, Leo Szilard, a scientist from Hungary, stepped off a curb in London to cross a street. By the time he got to the other side, he had glimpsed the future of nuclear energy six years before nuclear fission was discovered. It was a case of two (or more) of his neuron clusters joining up in his brain to suggest that if an element could be found that when one neutron (note the "t") is bombarded it would release two neutrons, it could lead to a chain reaction and the release of huge amounts of energy – call it a neuron explosion as well.[9]

Similarly with J.K. Rowling: "In 1990, while she was on a four-hour-delayed train trip from Manchester to London, the idea for a story of a young boy attending a school of wizardry 'came fully formed' into her mind."[10]

The Mind Never Sleeps

One under-appreciated power of the mind is that it is always working, as verified by many whose minds found solutions to problems while they slept.

Seeking to find a logical pattern for chemical elements, Dmitri Mendeleev wrote the name of each known element on cards together with its characteristics. Then he moved the cards around on a table seeking a consistent arrangement, one that could include elements yet to be discovered. Tired after many hours of trying, he fell asleep at his desk. He wrote, "In a dream I saw a table where all the elements fell into place as required. Awakening, I immediately wrote it down on a piece of paper."[11]

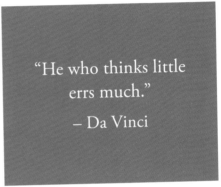

"He who thinks little errs much."

– Da Vinci

Thus we have the Periodic Table of Elements.

God created our minds to mimic His. **It is the instrument that first uses agency to envision and initiate action – the famous command to act.** Great mental powers await us in eternity as we learn to think deeply and tap into the source of all intelligence.

The glory of God, and therefore His power, is indeed intelligence.

❧

Orson Pratt visualized the mind we will have in the hereafter:

"Instead of thinking in one channel,
knowledge will rush in from all quarters; it will
come in light like the light which flows from the sun,
penetrating every part, informing the spirit, and
giving understanding concerning ten thousand things
at the same time; and the mind will be capable
of receiving and retaining all."[12]

Chapter 3

Inspiration
The Power of Pondering

"If Joseph Smith's transcendent experience in
the Sacred Grove teaches us anything, it is that the
heavens are open and that God speaks to His children."
— Russell M. Nelson

"The very nature of man requires him
to use his mind to capacity."
— Hugh Nibley

As we enjoy freedom and our minds expand,
we think both horizontally and vertically.

We have both radar and microscope.

The <u>curious</u> mind broadens the sweep of the
radar and produces numerous paths to explore.

The <u>pondering</u> mind uses the microscope to
pursue intriguing thoughts to greater depths.

Because deep discoveries do not come easily,
pursuing a single line of thought requires
<u>tolerance of uncertainty</u>.

Tolerance of uncertainty requires patience.

As patience increases, so too the ability to ponder.

Deep pondering leads to inspiration.

Ludwig van Beethoven would work in the morning and then retreat to his quiet space in the afternoon for two or three hours to let his mind delve deeply. Pencil and paper in hand, he would jot down thoughts and ideas.

His quiet space? He took walks. He "scribbled melodies and movements into a notebook during his daily walks through Vienna and the surrounding countryside. The walks broke up the intense work of composing and gave his mind room to wonder and take in inspiration from the world around."[1] To which I would add from the unseen world as well.

The practice led him, as an example, to write his Symphony No. 6, the famous Pastoral Symphony – the awakening of cheerful feelings on arrival in the countryside, sensations of the smell of blossoms, of grain fields after a storm, and the sounds of villagers enjoying themselves all brilliantly captured in music.

Walking and Thinking

Many accomplished composers, authors, and artists have discovered the power of walking for the quiet pondering time it affords – philosophers Goethe and Kant; authors Dickens and Milton; statesmen Churchill and Gandhi; scientists Einstein and Tesla; and Beethoven's fellow composers Schumann, Sibelius, and Tchaikovsky.

- As Schumann walked, "poems assumed melodic shape."

- Sibelius would walk the parks of Helsinki until he had composed a whole work, such as *Finlandia (Be Still, My Soul)*, in his head, and only then put it to paper.

- Tchaikovsky was such a dedicated walker (superstitious, he feared tragedy if he walked less than two hours a day) that he didn't care if rain drenched him.

- Nikola Tesla worked out the idea of alternating current while walking in a New York park.

- And for Beethoven, walks allowed him to incubate, evaluate, and reflect upon ideas.[2]

What did these noted men of accomplishment find so beneficial in walks?

First of all it's relaxing and changing scenery stimulates the playful mind. Call it *horizontal thinking* where the mind as a radar sweeps both mental and physical horizons to collect interesting combinations, new ideas, fun stuff. Playfully tinkering with sights and sounds of nature, we enjoy the excitement of serendipitous discovery.

Later in the walk, the mind tires of play and seeks meaning. It turns from radar to microscope and we have *vertical thinking*. We drill down. We push for deeper meaning and applications of the most promising ideas gathered from our radar. We seek inspiration and the "aha" clarity that completes the two-step flow of creativity.

> I tried to daydream, but my mind kept wandering.

For great composers and scientists, walking provided a break from routine and became a quiet space in nature conducive to the somber contemplation and meditation we call pondering, which in turn is connected to patience.

Patience – Stifle the Urge to Purge

Prospective astronauts are screened on decision-making ability. In one test, they are given a problem and must select one of four solutions within ten seconds. Most people, the examiners discovered, make a tentative choice in the first two seconds, use the next seven seconds to see if a different choice might be better, and then state their decision in the tenth second.

The problem is the quick choice sits in the back pocket of the would-be astronaut and, as the seconds tick down, morphs into the favored choice because one of the remaining options must be *significantly stronger* to displace it. All four choices are not given equal time and unbiased analysis.

> The impatient miss out on the fun of life.

Space agencies prefer the astronaut who will coolly give equal analysis to all possibilities over the full nine seconds – ignoring the urge to tentatively decide before thoroughly thinking – and make a decision in the tenth second.

As for us non-astronauts, the lesson is the same. The person who quickly decides may not only make a less-than-optimal choice, but miss the fun of life – checking everything out, imagining the outcomes, and in the process discovering connections not seen before. But we must persevere, just as Adam only received his answer "after many days."[3] Perhaps the Lord has to give us time to grow sufficient dendrites.

Speaking of which, dendrite growth will produce many seemingly ridiculous comparisons, but stifling the quick urge to purge builds patience, which in time may uncover disguised gems and produce the combinations that lead to creativity, learning, humor, and progress.

Famous movie director Alfred Hitchcock knew the value of patience, of waiting for ideas to form. One of his regular writers described working with him:

"When we came up against a block and our discussions became very heated and intense, Hitchcock would suddenly stop and tell a story that had nothing to do with the work at hand. At first, I was almost outraged, and then I discovered that he did this intentionally. *He mistrusted working under pressure.* He would say, 'We're pressing, we're pressing, we're working too hard. Relax, it will come.' And it always did."[4]

Berkeley psychology professor Donald MacKinnon "discovered that the most creative professionals always played with a problem for much longer before they tried to resolve it, because they were prepared to tolerate that slight discomfort and anxiety that we all experience when we haven't solved a problem."[5]

The full use of agency occurs when we are patient and allow the brain enough time to make comparisons between a new stimulus and other ideas already on the table.

The person who can be patient until all options have been equally and thoroughly explored will get the most out of life. He will be the one most likely to follow the Savior's example of patience ... and return to dwell in God's presence.

Tolerating Uncertainty

A free-ranging stimulus that hasn't yet found a friendly neuron cluster is uncomfortable for people who want an overly organized brain. I'm not arguing for sloppiness, but there is an advantage to mental clutter – tolerating something that "doesn't quite fit in as yet" long enough to figure out the best usefulness for that new piece of knowledge.

In fancy-speak terms, this is known as high dissonance tolerance.

Tolerating uncertainty long enough to really "check things out" distinguishes the deep from the shallow thinker. The greatest creative minds in history have been housed in high-dissonance-tolerance people, whereas those at the opposite end of the scale fear change and are less creative.

The high-dissonance-tolerance person will duly reflect on the total menu of comparisons, even those that may at first appear useless. Progress comes from tolerating the "uncertainty of the new" and remaining open long enough for the mind to generate ideas. The result is a person who is tolerant, open, cheerful, playful, curious, and **enjoys the resulting discoveries and new challenges.**

Einstein's whole career is an endorsement of the power of tolerance and patience:

"It's not that I'm so smart, but I stay with the questions much longer."

The low-dissonance-tolerance person, on the other hand, has the urge to purge stimuli and comparisons that don't yield immediate satisfaction. He spends less time testing for combinations. He crams the item into the first convenient "close enough" neuron cluster and slams the door. He thus becomes intolerant, closed, sour, lazy, suspicious, and **doesn't want new ways of looking at things for fear they will upset his settled worldviews.**

Pondering for the Aha

Sometimes the required depth of pondering is not measured in hours or days, but in years. Georg Friedrich Händel had been a composer for over 50 years before he was privileged to have his "aha" moment and produce *Messiah*, his most famous work. For 21 days in August of 1741, he composed upwards of 60 magnificent pieces the caliber of the *Hallelujah Chorus*, and such was the event that his assistant found him in tears saying, "I did think I saw heaven open, and saw the very face of God."[6]

Pondering is tenacious contemplation – focused deliberation and calm meditation. It takes concentration and effort, but it exponentially enhances and extends the creative process. Enjoy these observations:

Elder Neal A. Maxwell: "Pondering is much more than drifting or daydreaming, for it focuses and stirs us, not lulls us. … The length of time involved in pondering is not as important as the intensity given to it. Reflection cannot be achieved in the midst of distraction."[7]

Elder Joseph B. Wirthlin: "To soundly plant good seeds in your heart requires prolonged, intense, unremitting pondering. It is a deep, ongoing, regenerating process which refines the soul."[8]

President Joseph F. Smith: "As I pondered over these things which are written, the eyes of my understanding were opened, and the Spirit of the Lord rested upon me."[9]

Eric Hoffer in *The Ordeal of Change*: "The working out of ideas and insights requires persistent hard thinking, but the original insight is most likely to come when elements stored in different compartments of the mind drift into the open, jostle one another, and coalesce to form new combinations."

Nephi: For my soul delighteth in the scriptures, and <u>my heart</u> <u>pondereth them</u>, and writeth them for the learning and the profit of my children.[10]

And a direct commandment from the Savior after His instructions to the Nephites: "... ponder upon the things which I have said ..."[11]

There is a mechanism here. In some real and undeniable way, proper pondering moves us into a new dimension of understanding. We tap into a higher intellect, a higher way of thinking. We combine heart and mind. To use Elder Maxwell's verb, we are **stirred** to greater accomplishments, be they inventions, compositions, or literature to benefit mankind or personal refinement for our individual benefit.

So what's the formula? The simple advice of experts is to be alone in a peaceful place, perhaps your living room early in the morning before the kids wake up. Become **quiet in your mind.** Shut out worldly matters. Then think, meditate, reflect, mull, consider, wonder, and muse **deeply with mind and heart.**

When we push ourselves to ponder deeply, we tap into more and more neuron clusters already in our brain. If persistently pursued, exhaustively if needed, the Lord then rewards our preparatory thinking and forms new clusters in our brain. **Inspiration – clear thoughts that feel right.** Thus the aha moments when something beyond brain power feeds the mind.

> "The best thinking has been done in solitude. The worst has been done in turmoil."
>
> – Edison

It's available to all of God's children, even those who don't recognize the Source. Vladimir Nabokov, an agnostic, described it as a "prefatory glow" that leads to a feeling of "tickly well-being" allowing a writer such as himself to "forefeel" what he is going to write.

Others have compared it to a gust of wind, a new way of seeing, something greater than themselves, powerful but fleeting. The word itself comes from the Latin *inspirare*, meaning "to breathe into."[12]

And who does the "breathing into" ...?

Prophets, Pruning, Promptings

President Russell M. Nelson keeps pencil and paper near his bed to capture promptings and insights that come when the mind is at rest. This ties in with what neuroscientists are discovering. When we are asleep, the brain's gardeners – known as microglial cells – do the pruning and clear the day's clutter. They eliminate less-used neural connections thus opening more brain space for new thoughts and ideas when we are just waking up. Isn't it logical that God might use those hours to deliver inspiration?

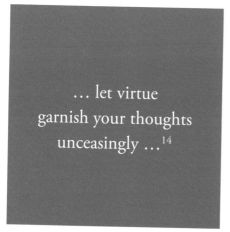

... let virtue garnish your thoughts unceasingly ...[14]

The process builds upon itself. A newly pruned mind at rest invites inspiration which in turn encourages further cleansing of the unimportant, the dross. It is power and if patiently allowed to work, will clean up improper neuron clusters and pathways.

The brain's delete button was described in a 2016 article: "To take advantage of your brain's natural gardening system, **simply think about the things that are important to you.** Your gardeners will strengthen those connections and prune the ones that you care about less."[13]

As we use this system to control our minds and purify our thoughts, two types of guidance come from the Holy Ghost. Elder Richard G. Scott explained:

> "When it is crisp and clear and essential, it warrants the title of *revelation*. When it is a series of promptings we often have to guide us step by step to a worthy objective ... it is *inspiration*."[15]

Confirming the mental opportunities as we awaken, he also said:

> "Revelation can also be given in a dream when there is an almost imperceptible transition from sleep to wakefulness. If you strive to capture the content immediately, you can record great detail, but otherwise it fades rapidly. Inspired communication in the night is generally accompanied by a sacred feeling for the entire experience. ... Two indicators that a feeling or prompting comes from God are that it produces peace in your heart and a quiet, warm feeling."

The word "quicken" is often used to explain how the Holy Ghost adds clarity and depth to our mental efforts. Elder Keith K. Hilbig elaborated:

> "When we invite the Holy Ghost to fill our minds with light and knowledge, He 'quickens' us, that is to say, enlightens and enlivens the inner man or woman. ... We feel strengthened, filled with peace and joy ... spiritual energy and enthusiasm ...."[16]

Light, warmth, joy, a "makes sense" feeling. Note also the connection between Elder Scott's advice to write it down, President Nelson's habit of writing it down, and Beethoven's practice of taking notes while walking.

こ

After Moroni's third visit to Joseph Smith that memorable night
of September 21-22, 1823, he said he "was again left to ponder."
After three visits from a heavenly messenger,
how could one do anything but?

Chapter 4

Humor
Unexpected Connections

"A sense of humor is an escape valve
for the pressures of life."

– Richard G. Scott

A fertile mind produces humor
and humor returns the favor.

The greater the agency,
the more we think.

The more we think,
the more choices we discover.

The more the choices,
the more comparisons we make.

The more comparisons,
the more the connections.

The more connections,
the more incongruous some will be.

Unexpected, incongruous connections
are the essence of humor.

Think long enough
and you will find something funny.

Therefore, the stronger the agency,
the more we laugh and enjoy life.

Though Benjamin Franklin was the pre-eminent American statesman of the 1770s, some Founding Fathers opposed tasking him to write the Declaration of Independence. They were afraid he would insert a joke and the colonists wouldn't be taken seriously.

Same with Abraham Lincoln. Organizers of the historic Gettysburg ceremony initially balked at inviting him to deliver remarks "because they feared he would try to say something funny."[1]

Benjamin Franklin and Abraham Lincoln were both horizontal and vertical thinkers. They had playful minds housed in high-dissonance-tolerance bodies faced with monumental tasks. But they knew when and how to use humor to good effect.

I believe the Savior Himself has a delightful sense of humor. Take the incident when he chastised Pharisees for being so blindly committed to picky law that they "strain at a gnat and swallow a camel."[2] It's a stretch for an English speaker to connect those two items, other than something small to contrast against something big. But in Aramaic, it was a play on words that fit with the culture. In the Savior's native language, a gnat is *gamla* and a camel is *gamal*.[3]

> Tweet others as you would like to be tweeted.

So by switching two letters, the Savior not only ridiculed the Pharisees but did so with a first-class pun that had to have sparked laughter. And those who exercise unrighteous power cannot stand to be laughed at.

Humor of the Prophets

The Prophet Joseph Smith described himself as having a "cheerful disposition." And so it is with recent prophets.

President Gordon B. Hinckley:

> "After my closing remarks, the choir will sing, 'Where Can I Turn for Peace?' (Slight pause) Who chooses these hymns anyway?"

> At the dedication of the BYU Alumni Center named in his honor: "Normally they don't name buildings for people who are still alive, but in this case they thought half-dead was good enough."[4]

President Spencer W. Kimball:[5]

> After an operation on his vocal chords, which caused him a great deal of pain and sleeplessness, he complained, "Insomnia is my trouble. Why, I couldn't even doze in sacrament meeting yesterday."

> Encouraged to take some aspirin for pain, he said, "I don't want to take any more pills; I'm already the 'piller' of the Church."

President David O. McKay:

> "Let husband and wife never speak to one another in loud tones, unless the house is on fire."[6]

> He pitied those who couldn't laugh. "I feel a little sorry for those who have such long faces that they have to sleep on their pillow lengthwise."[7]

Gentle humor. The chuckle, not the guffaw.

❧

A Special Part of the Brain

Yes, we know that the left inferior frontal gyrus is the region of the brain that grasps the connection between incongruous elements at the heart of a joke. But somehow that tidbit of knowledge doesn't make us laugh.

These unexpected connections and surprise endings, however, might. Courtesy of Steven Wright ...

The early bird gets the worm, but the second mouse gets the cheese.

If at first you don't succeed, then skydiving is definitely not for you.

I spilled spot remover on my dog. Now he's gone.

Don't worry if you can't spell Armageddon; it's not the end of the world.

I used to work in a fire hydrant factory. Could never find a place to park.

What if there were no hypothetical situations?

Don't worry if Plan A fails; there are 25 more letters in the alphabet.

Let chickens cross the road and don't question their motives.

Before you criticize someone, walk a mile in their shoes. That way, you'll be a mile from them and you'll have their shoes.

If Cinderella's shoe fit perfectly, why did it fall off?

Why pay money to have your family tree traced; go into politics and your opponents will do it for you.

Toes are smarter than brains; they can find furniture in the dark.

Someone who studies earthquakes is a fault-finder.

If you can smile when things go wrong, you have someone in mind to blame.

And in the same vein:

If you worked for a company that manufactured kitchen counters, and if you worked hard, would you become counter productive?

A boy asks his mom, "Why are grandma and grandpa always reading the Bible?" The mother replies, "Well, grandma is cramming for finals and grandpa is looking for loopholes."

"I can hardly wait until tomorrow because I get better looking every day." "Given how old you are, what did you look like when you started?"

As the duck said to the Chapstick salesman, "Put it on my bill."

Ah, humor and the wonderful brain that never sleeps. It is active 24/7 from the moment we're born until the day we fall in love.

Humor About Church Culture

In the tradition of Jeff Foxworthy ("you might be a redneck if ..."), why not a bit of self-deprecating humor?

You might be a Latter-day Saint ...

If 18-year-olds in your church are called elders.

If 85% of your full-time missionaries are teenagers.

If your church has something called Fast Sunday, and it's anything but.

If your food storage is older than your children.

If all your serving bowls have tape on the bottom with your name on them.

If you know what it means to serve funeral potatoes at a wedding.

If you buy a box of Cheerios and eat less than half of it at home.

If you hear beehives are having a party … with deacons … and it makes perfect sense. [Too bad we won't have beehives any more.]

And … if you can name the middle initials of the top 15 leaders of your church, … then you are definitely a Latter-day Saint.

"We've got to have a little humor in our lives," said President Gordon B. Hinckley. "You had better take seriously that which should be taken seriously but, at the same time, we can bring in a touch of humor now and again. If the time ever comes when we can't smile at ourselves, it will be a sad time."[8]

Humor Amid Repression

Agency spawns humor and humor in return protects agency because tyrants cannot stand to be laughed at. Hitler, for instance, set up "joke courts" to punish those who named horses and dogs Adolf.[9]

A mind with ample dendrites can find humor in anything, anywhere. Russian writer Andrei Sinyavsky observes, "No matter how much the anecdote is suppressed (in my time you could get from five to ten years for telling one – imagine: for words!), it only gets strength from this suppression – not the strength of malice, but of humor and sunshine."[10]

Here are a few from that time when, under Article 58 of the Penal Code, certain jokes might be judged anti-Soviet propaganda and a capital offense:[11]

> A man calls up the KGB and says, "My parrot flew out the window. If you guys happen to find it, please remember that I do not share its views."

> A Soviet judge walks out of his chambers laughing hysterically. A colleague asks him why he's laughing. "I just heard the funniest joke in the world." "Well, go ahead, tell me," says the other judge. "I can't – I just gave someone ten years for it."

> A citizen called a government minister an idiot and was sentenced to 15 years at hard labor. He wasn't sentenced for slander; he was sentenced for revealing a state secret.

> A Soviet citizen makes a down payment on a new car and asks how long before delivery. "Precisely ten years from today." "Will that be morning or afternoon?" "Why, what difference does it make?" "Well, the plumber's coming in the morning."

> Citizen Rabinowitz showed up at the May Day demonstration with a placard that read: Thank You Comrade Stalin for My Happy Childhood. "What's the matter with you, old man? Why, when you were a child, Comrade Stalin hadn't even been born." "That's what I'm thankful for."

After surviving the Nazi death camp at Auschwitz, psychiatrist Viktor Frankl wrote, "Humor was another of the soul's weapons in the fight for self-preservation. ... Humor more than anything else in the human make-up can afford an aloofness and an ability to rise above any situation, if only for a few seconds."[12]

Even in a concentration camp, the mind has agency. It uses its freedom of choices – the imagination – to tinker with new combinations and perhaps discover solutions and paths of action. Egged on by laughter.

The attempted suppression of humor in totalitarian regimes says volumes about agency and the power of laughter as we continue our journey back home.

ℛ

Think about our spirit siblings who decided not to come on this earthly trip. Can you imagine that they enjoy humor as we do? They undoubtedly bandy about ridicule, mocking laughter, sarcasm and sardonic attempts at cleverness, but genuine, gentle, pure humor? I think not.

> "Don't be afraid to laugh.
> A person without a sense of humor
> misses much of the joy of living."
> – David O. McKay

Chapter 5

Power
What It's All About

"Nearly all men can stand adversity, but if you want to test a man's character, give him power."
– Abraham Lincoln

Here in our second estate, the test is not only
how we use power in our individual dealings with others,
but also how combined power is used in our behalf or against us
as members of a group or as citizens of a nation.

Power is the ability to act;
it is the authority to act.

It is central to our progress.

God has given us power/energy.

He desires to share His power/authority with us.

Through His gift of agency we learn
how to use power correctly.

We learn to use it in individual settings.

We learn to use it as part of
a group, organization, or nation.

Power freely and righteously exercised
leads to progress; otherwise tyranny.

As we use power wisely, we progress
and become more like God.

No blessing comes from God
save it be through proper exercise of
the powers He has entrusted to us.

As we achieve, we add to God's honor
and therefore His power.

An Indian folk tale tells of a wise woman who could predict the weather, heal the sick with herbs, and resolve arguments. Some children in the village decided to test her renowned abilities and went to her home. Holding a bird behind his back, one of them, intending to either kill it or let it fly away depending on the answer he received, said, "I'm holding a bird behind my back. Is it alive or dead?"

She perceptively answered, "It's all in your hands."

Same with the power that comes with agency. It's all in our hands.

⁜

Power and Powers

With rudimentary agency in our pre-earthly existence, we could think, move, talk. We could choose to play heavenly sports, attend heavenly socials, or take earth prep classes. We could act, but had limited capacity. Further, we knew of the Father's power. We saw His creations, we listened to His powerful teachings, we yearned to become as He is.

While robust agency had to wait until freedom and power could be practiced in an earthly state with the capacities of an earthly body, our first significant test of agency happened before we received that mortal body. We had to choose sides when we witnessed one of the Father's highly ranked sons start a war over ... power.

> Behold, here am I, send me, I will be thy son, and I will redeem all mankind, that one soul shall not be lost, and surely I will do it; wherefore give me thine honor.[1]

Some might think the honor Lucifer wanted was recognition or thanks or a "way to go, Luce" pat on the back, but it was not. What Satan meant by "thine honor" is explained in an 1830 revelation:

> [Satan] rebelled against me, saying, Give me thine honor, **which is my power**; and also a third part of the hosts of heaven turned he away from me because of their agency.[2]

Power. That's what it was all about then and what it is all about today, this key component of agency central to our path to exaltation. And to make sure Lucifer knew the pecking order, and as an indicator of the power God shared with Jehovah, the Father Himself did not kick Satan out. He tasked the Savior to do the job:

> Wherefore, because that Satan rebelled against me, and sought to destroy the agency of man, which I, the Lord God, had given him, and also, that I should give unto him mine own power; **by the power of mine Only Begotten**, I caused that he should be cast down ....[3]

Satan did not want to *share* in the Father's power. He wanted to *displace* Him and have it all. Still does.

Our spiritual siblings who chose Lucifer's plan feared failing the trials of power and agency. Lucifer promised that all would return and the poor souls believed it.

We, on the other hand, have the opportunity to receive all that God has. He wants to share His power with us so we can learn to handle it properly and become as He is. As we follow God's commandments, we honor Him. In other words, our progress brings Him more power. Sharing brings increase.

To these magnificent win-win ends, consider the powers God has given or wants to give us:

Power of agency

Power of a spirit body

Power of a mortal body

Power of procreation

Power of knowledge

Power of scriptures

Power of the Savior's gospel, teachings, example

Power of the Savior's Atonement

Power of the priesthood

Power of the gift of the Holy Ghost

Power of the endowment

Power of repentance

Power of thrones, kingdoms, principalities, dominions

Power of the continuation of seed forever

Power of eternal progression

Power of exaltation

To these we must add powers beyond our present ability to comprehend and not yet revealed.

Now list the helpful powers Satan wants us to have ......

Go ahead; I'm waiting.

Power as Ability to Act

After the Grand Council and our vote, at which there were no abstentions,[4] we entered earth life with mortal bodies, a full measure of agency to choose and use power, no recollection of our life before, and an adversary bent on our destruction. A test, to say the least.

> [Men] should be anxiously engaged in a good cause, and do many things of their own free will, and bring to pass much righteousness; For the **power** is in them, wherein they are **agents unto themselves**.[5]

We have energy, we have ability, and we have the judgment to do many things of our own free will, to decide by ourselves our own course of action knowing that the Lord will not command in all things. The Savior is the example. We may not have power flowing from our robes to heal a woman who touches the hem, but we can act as He acted. We do have our own level of power. Our deeds rarely compare, but one story comes close.

When a concentration camp prisoner escaped from Auschwitz in July 1941, the Nazi commandant picked ten men to be starved to death to deter further escapes. One of the selected men cried out, "My wife! My children!" Maximilian Kolbe, a 47-year-old Polish priest volunteered to take his place! He died two weeks later. Greater love hath no man … nor more mature agency.[6]

We have numerous opportunities to help or hurt a fellow child of God by the way we employ the power of our agency. The little tests of life that add up. The commandant at Auschwitz, Karl Fritzsch, who consigned ten innocent men to death undoubtedly felt justified. He now knows the other side of the agency coin.

Power as Authority to Act

We have the *ability* to act, so why shouldn't the *authority* to act come with it?

It actually does for the things we personally want to accomplish, but special permission is required of the things the Lord wants to accomplish. We can act in our *own* name however we choose, but we need the authority of the priesthood to act in *Christ's* name, to direct *His* work according to *His* will.

President Thomas S. Monson:

> "The priesthood is not really so much a gift as it is a commission to serve, a privilege to lift, and an opportunity to **bless the lives of others.**"[7]

Note the last phrase. All of us can help others and do so as fallible yet caring humans, but to have the authority to go beyond that and tap into heavenly powers to help others is a humbling concept. Staggering even. And yet it is part of God's plan for special assistance from heaven to bring about the His purposes and prepare us for the Second Coming.

The special authority to act exists only to help others by calling down, as in blessings on the sick, the healing powers of heaven. A holder of the true priesthood cannot use it for selfish purposes, as pretenders do by wearing fine robes, crowns, capes and bandying about titles and honorifics.

> That they [the rights of the priesthood] may be conferred upon us, it is true; but when we undertake to cover our sins, or to gratify our pride, our vain ambition, or to exercise control or dominion or compulsion upon the souls of the children of men, in any degree of unrighteousness, behold, the heavens withdraw themselves; the Spirit of the Lord is grieved; and when it is withdrawn, Amen to the priesthood or the **authority** of that man.[8]

Ever seen a priesthood holder lay his hands on his own head and give himself a blessing?

Power as a Problem

Agency wouldn't be agency without the freedom and the power to think, choose, move, and act. Power is, was, and always will be a magnet – attractive, desirable, useful, but also potentially dangerous.

The challenge throughout history has been how to give leaders the right amount of power to accomplish good for their nations, societies or tribes, but not so much that they become tyrants. Kings, czars, and potentates were the rule of the day for millennia and one could only hope for benevolent ones. The scorecard hasn't been pretty.

> Therefore, if it were possible that you could have just men to be your kings, who would establish the laws of God ... then it would be expedient ... (but) because all men are not just it is not expedient that ye should have a king or kings to rule over you.[9]

Short of having a just and righteous king (a rarity indeed), how should we control governmental power?

Over the centuries, several societies established representative governments to better control how power is exercised – Athens with its pure democracy in the fifth century BC, the Roman Republic with its Senate for 500 years before Caesar took dictatorial powers, the Dutch Republic breaking away from Spain in the late 1500s, and various more localized experiments such as the Italian city states and the cities of the Hanseatic League.

Astute philosophers – Aristotle, Montesquieu, Montaigne, Locke – proposed ideas such as checks and balances, and the separation of powers, but the underlying practice never varied: government, however formed, was sovereign over the people, and people's rights, if any, came from government.

No significant power rearrangement, grounded in a constitution as foundational law, happened until the last quarter of the 18th century. Because coming events of the Restoration required a power environment more conducive to individual agency, things had to be different. The gospel could not be restored in a nation conditioned to cave to the whims of whoever claimed the DNA of an ancestor who fobbed onto the huddled masses that his power grab was God's will – the "Divine Right of Kings" blasphemy.

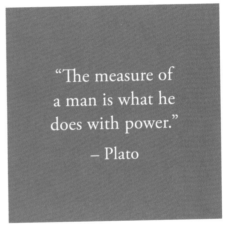

"The measure of a man is what he does with power."
– Plato

It began with the Declaration of Independence:

> "We hold these truths to be self-evident, that all men are created equal, that they are endowed by their Creator with certain unalienable Rights, that among these are Life, liberty and the pursuit of Happiness. That to secure these rights, Governments are instituted among Men, **deriving their just powers from the consent of the governed.**"

Then came the Constitution of the United States of America – that brilliant departure from history's sad story.

> According to the laws and constitution of the people, which I have suffered to be established, and should be maintained for the rights and protection of all flesh...
>
> That every man may act ... **according to the moral agency** which I have given unto him, that every man may be **accountable** for his own sins ...
>
> Therefore, it is not right that any man should be in bondage one to another.
>
> And for this purpose have I established the Constitution of this land, by the hands of wise men whom I raised up unto this very purpose ....[10]

God has <u>inspired</u> people to do numerous good things through the centuries, but less often has He <u>established</u> things through wise men raised up to that very purpose – the discovery of America, the Constitution, and the re-establishment of original Christianity being chief among those impacting latter-day lives.

The Constitution changes the way we <u>think</u> about power and government:

- The people are sovereign; government is the servant. Thomas Jefferson said it was the first time in history that this has happened. How could such an earth-jarring departure from the customary people-government relationship have been implemented if not from God?

- Our rights come from God, not from government. The foundational "inalienable rights" are life, liberty and the pursuit of happiness, the last of which has been defined (by John Locke and others) as the right to own one's labor and thus the fruits thereof.

- Government's duty is to protect those rights, not restrict or redefine them to its benefit.

Then come the three famous mechanisms how power must be handled in a secular world:

- <u>Separate</u> the powers between three equal branches of government – legislative, executive, and judicial.

- <u>Divide</u> the powers between the federal government and the state governments.

- <u>Enumerate</u> the powers – 18 specific powers belong to the federal government, all others belong to the states and/or the people. That America's government has increased its powers beyond these specific ones, using imaginative interpretations of the General Welfare clause and the Necessary and Proper clause, is all too painfully clear.

Do we fully appreciate how revolutionary these concepts are for the control of power?

❧

"We have staked the whole future of our new nation,
not upon the power of government; far from it. We have staked
the future of all our political constitutions upon the capacity of
each of ourselves to **govern ourselves** according to the moral
principles of the Ten Commandments of God."

– James Madison

Chapter 6

Obey

Submitting Our Agency
to the Father's Will

"We made vows, solemn vows, in the heavens
before we came to this mortal life."
— Spencer W. Kimball

What manner of man is this
that even the winds and the sea obey him![1]

Agency gives us the freedom
to choose good or evil.

Our choice of good over evil
becomes a formal commitment when
we enter into covenants with the Father.

The highest level of obedience
is the covenant sealed by an oath.

Just as we make covenants here on earth,
we also made covenants before we came here.

In our pre-earthly state we covenanted to
be obedient and to submit our agency – our
sovereignty over self – to the will of the Father.

Counterintuitive as it may seem,
we enhance our agency by surrendering it
to the will of the Father.

Through such submission
we gain power.

A rmed with the latest weaponry, two armies – maybe two or three divisions on each side – faced each other in battle.

After days of ferocious fighting, one exhausted side surrendered. In an unbelievable gesture, the commander of the victorious army told these prisoners of war they could go back to their homes if they would simply promise never to return to battle again. Say a few words and avoid a POW compound.

Realizing their plight, the defeated soldiers gave their promise, bitter though the battle had been. They departed in peace. They were men of their word and never again came to war.

What kind of people would have such a history of **obedience to their oaths** that even centuries-long enemies would be confident they wouldn't betray an agreement?

Lamanites and Nephites, that's who.[2]

Covenants – To Cut an Agreement

A few years later, Captain Moroni, who had defeated Zarahemnah and the Lamanites, returned to his home. There soon arose dissenters among his own people who were "**exceedingly wroth**" (what a phrase) against their brethren "**insomuch as they were determined to slay them.**"[3]

Enough's enough, thought Captain Moroni, so he … rent his coat?

Some people think he just needed a piece of cloth so he could write something on it and hoist a title of liberty.[4] No, it was more than a piece of cloth.

He ripped his *coat* as a demonstration of a *covenant*.

In the Old Testament world and the ancient American continent, to make a covenant under the law of Moses meant to tear flesh. Two people would agree on something and as a symbol would sacrifice an animal and cut it, each contracting party receiving half. It had to be something of value. The cutting of flesh in the circumcision covenant was, of course, symbolic of and a similitude of the Lord's coming sacrifice. In fact, the Hebrew word for covenant is *berith*, which derives from the root "to cut."[5] (And that's where we get our English phrase "to cut a deal.")

So when Captain Moroni rent his coat he was really signaling "I'm going to make a covenant and I invite the rest of you to join me." They came running together and did just that. The people even rent their own garments as a token or as a covenant that they would not fall into transgression, but would keep the commandments and preserve liberty.[6]

Even the Elements Had Agency and Made Covenants

Not many people in today's world, from any nation, honor their promises under all conditions. But earthly elements do.

Consider these scriptures from the Book of Abraham:[7]

- And the Gods ordered … the waters under the heaven be gathered together … and let the earth come up dry … and the Gods saw that they were <u>obeyed</u>.

- And the Gods organized the earth to bring forth grass … seed … herb … tree … fruit … and the Gods saw that they were <u>obeyed</u>.

- And the Gods watched those things which they had ordered until they <u>obeyed</u>.

If the Gods ordered, organized, and watched *until* they were obeyed, it implies there was a time period in which the elements had two choices – obey or not obey. Which in turn implies the elements had ... agency.

Not just *had* agency, they have agency, but it is now enhanced (let's add the word *enjoyed*) by the covenants they made to the Gods. Even down to the molecular level, as noted in D&C 88:

> ... we truly can command in the name of Jesus and the very trees obey us ....[8]

The earth abides the law of a celestial kingdom, for it fills the measure of its creation, and transgresses not the law. Wherefore it shall be sanctified; yea, notwithstanding it shall die, it shall be quickened again, and shall abide the power by which it is quickened, and the righteous shall inherit it.[9]

Elder John A. Widtsoe commented on this passage:

"If the earth is a living organism, it seems more than likely that **all things on earth possess a measure of life and intelligence**."[10]

Hugh Nibley in a 1980 address said that what the Gods ordered "was not the completed product, but the process to bring [the creation] about, providing a scheme under which life might expand: 'Let us prepare the earth to bring forth grass' not 'Let us *create* grass.'[11] ... 'They obeyed' is the active voice .... Everybody gets into the act. Every creature, to the limit of its competence, is given the supreme compliment of being left on its own, so that the word 'obey' is correctly applied."[12]

If the mountains and the oceans and all creatures are smart enough to obey, why not we?

Pre-Mortal Covenants

The scriptures speak about **foreordinations** – an obvious ceremony that took place in the spirit world that had to have involved an agreement or covenant. Certain noble and great ones were chosen to be God's rulers – prophets and apostles, such as Abraham.[13]

> And if a person gains more knowledge and intelligence in this life through his diligence and **obedience** than another, he will have so much the advantage in the world to come.[14]

It seems to follow that other people were ordained to whatever offices they would hold on earth. Such has been indicated in more than one patriarchal blessing.

President Dallin H. Oaks:

"All of the myriads of mortals who have been born on this earth chose the Father's plan and fought for it. Many of us also made covenants with the Father concerning what we would do in mortality. In ways that have not been revealed, **our actions in the spirit world influence us in mortality**."[15]

That more than one covenant was made between God and us before we came here has been touched upon by latter-day prophets. Elder Neal A. Maxwell states:

"Elder Orson Hyde said of our life in the premortal world, 'We understood things better there than we do in this lower world.' He also surmised as to the agreements we made there that 'it is not impossible that we signed the articles thereof with our own hands – which articles may be retained in the archives above, to be presented to us when we rise from the dead, and be judged out of our own mouths, according to that which is written in the books.' Just because we have forgotten, said Elder Hyde, 'our forgetfulness cannot alter the facts.' Hence, the **degree of detail** involved in the covenants and promises we participated in at that time may be a **more highly customized** thing than many of us surmise."[16]

Obedience to Divine Law

One year before he became the 17th President of the Church, President Russell M. Nelson gave a significant and memorable address at a Worldwide Devotional for Young Adults in which he powerfully explained divine law and obedience. Three key paragraphs:

"Divine law is incontrovertible and irrefutable. Divine law cannot be denied or disputed. And when God's laws are obeyed, relevant blessings *always* result! Blessings are always predicated upon obedience to applicable law.[17]

"Existentialists can expound; relativists can rationalize with their constricted views of reality – that truth is only a subjective experience. But God's laws are laws. God's truth is really true! What God says is right *is* right! And what He says is wrong *is* wrong!

"That is why it is imperative that you know God's laws. They control this universe and multitudes of others. When divine laws are broken, consequences follow. Even though our hearts ache for those who break God's laws, penalties must be paid. Divine law must be obeyed."[18] [His emphases]

Definition, Purpose, Freedom, Rights

Misunderstandings about agency are sometimes caused by confusing definition and purpose. Agency as a *definition* obviously includes the freedom to choose either good or evil, to be our own agent and run our own life. The *purpose* of agency, on the other hand, is considerably deeper and takes on greater significance once we subject our agency to the Father's will by making covenants.

"We have not been blessed with moral agency to do whatever we want whenever we will," explained Elder David A. Bednar. "Rather, according to the Father's plan **we have received moral agency to choose the right**, to do good, and to become whatever God intends for us to become."[19]

He elaborated:

> "You and I exercise agency in the making of a covenant. When we enter into a covenant with God, we voluntarily surrender a portion of our agency. And the consequences that come from violating the covenant are not within our control. ... Agency is linked to a course of choosing the right. That is why we have agency. ... Agency is to be used in choosing the right."[20]

Agency in its full sense is the **right and power to achieve exaltation**.

We use our agency to submit to the will of the Father, just as did His Son.

In a sense, we can compare agency with a pile of money. We are free to spend it however we want, but the only way it will grow is if we invest it – surrender a portion of it – and follow the guidance of an all-knowing Financial Adviser. All other "investments" such as the enticements of the world will eat up our cash and come to naught.

In sum:

If we keep our covenants,
we will receive all that the Father has.[21]

Logically, that must include power
because we will have learned
to use it properly.

So as we obey,
we receive more power.

As we receive more power,
we have more freedom.

Obedience is not limiting;
it is liberating.

✐

"Mortality, then, is the time to test our ability to
understand our Heavenly Father's plan and, of course,
our willingness to be obedient. Obedience is essential to
obtaining exaltation and eternal life."
– M. Russell Ballard

Chapter 7

Choose
The Miracle of Menus

"Freedom of choice is more to be treasured
than any possession earth can give."
– David O. McKay

We have pinged our brain for ideas and are leaning toward a course of action.
As we try to visualize the consequences, hopes and fears enter the picture.
With logic of the mind and feelings of the heart, we decide our plan.

Choosing is the mental and emotional assessment of risk.

With dendrites and neurons
doing their jobs, we have the
horizontal playful mind.

With the pursuit of deeper meaning,
we have the vertical pondering mind.

With options lined up before us,
we have the deciding mind.

Without alternatives there is no agency.

With freedom to choose, we stand at
a critical test of self-ownership.

We can ask for advice, but
no one else can make the decision
save we lose agency.

As the Soviet Union crumbled, a political foundation invited budding young politicians from various parts of that empire to visit America to learn how we campaign in a multi-party system. A colleague and I took a few of them to lunch at a local restaurant.

The menu overwhelmed them. One young lady from Kazakhstan, very intelligent and fluent in English, was baffled by so many choices and didn't know what to select. The waitress arrived just then and hearing the problem said, "Let's start with the main dish – would you like chicken, beef or fish?"

"Uh, fish."

"White or pink?"

"Uh, white."

"Would you like halibut, tilapia or cod?

"Okay, uh, … the first one."

"Would you like soup or salad with that?"

"Uh, soup."

"Would you like French onion, mushroom, clam chowder, vegetable, or cream of chicken?"

"Uh, I changed my mind. I'll just have the salad."

"For the dressing, would you like ranch, thousand island, Italian, blue cheese, French, honey mustard, or raspberry vinaigrette?"

She randomly chose one, slumped and said, "I'm not used to that many choices. I'm exhausted."

If you don't have choices, you don't have agency. She found out that day what an agency-rich country she was visiting.

&

The Menu Upstairs

When someone seems puzzled by our use of the word *agency*, I suggest such synonyms as *free will* and *free to choose*. So stated, choice seems to be almost universally understood and is a good springboard for deeper conversation about the gift of agency, especially that this freedom to choose began before we were born.

The menu in our pre-earthly existence presented only two choices but the ingredients were exhaustively described and their impact vigorously debated. For us who chose the Father's offer, five ingredients were particularly tasty:

First, we trusted the Father. His power transformed us from intelligences into spirit sons and daughters. We could review our *past* progress, so we trusted His plan for our *future* progress.

Second, we believed His promises. This scripture given to us here was surely given to us there: "Eye hath not seen, nor ear heard, neither have entered into the heart of man, the things which God hath prepared for them that love him."[1] Even with our spiritual neurons firing explosively in such a fertile environment, our imagination up there was still insufficient to grasp all the Father has planned for us. But we knew the rewards must be fantastic.

Third, we had the promise of the Savior's Atonement. When He said He would come and sacrifice His life for us, it was as good as if it had already happened.

Fourth, we analyzed the consequences. We entertained a cost-benefit analysis and asked, "What consequences do I want to enjoy at the end of my earthly existence?" We figured out that rewards cannot and never will be obtained without risk, without action, without a cost. And we resolved to pay whatever price earth life might require of us.

Fifth, we became suspicious of Lucifer's rosy promises. In Earth Prep 101, we figured out why effort, problems, and opposition in all things had to be indispensable ingredients in the recipe for success, for exaltation. We grasped intuitively that nothing good can come without effort – that there is no free lunch, even in heaven. Lucifer's "trust-me-Harold" plan, on the other hand, reeked of "It's freeeeee!" Lucifer's followers simply thought they could get the goodies without the effort.

Whether we select from rich or paltry menus as we face decisions here on earth, the dynamics that launched us into mortality play the same role today. As we decide how we will proceed in any given situation, the question before us must always be: Does my menu choice *enhance* or *diminish* agency – help or hurt, promote or stifle individual progress?

The Acceleration Dynamic

Choosing whether to be open or closed to a possibility sparks a multiplier effect or acceleration factor. After Amulek shook Zeezrom into realizing his predicament, Alma explained the dynamic as applied to the mysteries of God:

> ... he that will not harden his heart, to him is given the greater portion of the word, until it is given unto him to know the mysteries of God **until he know them in full**.

> And they that will harden their hearts to them is given the lesser portion of the word **until they know nothing** concerning his mysteries ....[2]

More leads to more and less leads to less.

And not just the mysteries of God (which are all inclusive anyway). It's the same mind-pinging principle spoken of earlier whether applied to physics, medicine, chemistry, finance, the social sciences, you name it. The open mind, infused with agency and aided by a willing heart, sends tinker-feelers to other neurons to test for possible connections. One connection leads to another and then another as knowledge multiplies on itself. Under the opposite conditions, the mind and heart wither.

Openness of heart – willingness to consider – leads to accelerated knowledge whereas lack thereof leads to accelerated ignorance.

Many the Menus of Mortality

We naturally hesitate when we first see a new restaurant's menu. We may be excited to try something different but fear being disappointed. We ask others in our party what they're going to order and may ask questions of the waitress – the assessment phase. We then decide, if only as an experiment. Whether we ever order it again depends on the consequences.

> The more numerous the choices, the greater the chance for success. When choices are few, failure is more likely.

It is agency in practice: think, assess risks, choose, experience consequences, learn, and progress.

So it is with life's menus. Elder Neal A. Maxwell put it succinctly in four questions:

"Since we are here to thus be proved, how can that occur except we are tested? If we are here to learn to choose wisely, how can that occur except there be alternatives? If our soul is to be stretched, how can that happen without growing pains? How can personal development really occur amid routine unless we have **authentic challenges** on which to practice?"[3]

How can we learn "except there be alternatives" and "growing pains?" The essence of choosing is evaluating risk and determining one's tolerance for what may follow. **Risk-free progress no more exists than risk-free investments.**

Consider the counsel from three of our leaders:

President Thomas S. Monson: "With the *right* of choice comes the *responsibility* to choose."

President James E. Faust: "Some of our important choices have a time line. If we delay a decision, the opportunity is gone forever. Sometimes our doubts keep us from making a choice that involves change. Thus an opportunity may be missed."

President Russell M. Nelson: "[The Lord] must be the very foundation of your faith, and the testing of that faith is a fundamental reason for your freedom to choose."[4]

This may be grist for debate, but I submit we require and benefit from a more enhanced agency here on earth than we had in our pre-earthly existence.

We have the same power to think and choose here as we did there. But the decisions made in the pre-earthly existence happened as we lived with the Father. How much more difficult they are on earth without that memory; greater utilization of agency is required to conquer earthly trials.

Bear in mind as well that we are agents unto ourselves with powers here on earth we did not have or exercise previously: the power of a physical body, the power of procreation, the power of repentance, the power of the Savior's Atonement, and all the other powers noted in Chapter 5.

Hence, agency is enhanced by virtue of the conditions under which we make decisions and live with the consequences. Making decisions here on earth strengthens our confidence in being owners of ourselves, and choosing and then acting builds self-confidence which in turn leads to self-reliance and independence.

As we do, we realize we must use agency to obey truth. To counter this, states Elder Richard G. Scott, "Satan strives to persuade us to live outside the truth by rationalizing our actions as the right of choice."[5]

The Basic Menu ... Again

Over time we establish a decision-making pattern as we make choices, all of which cumulate into the most important decision we make in life:

> [Men] are **free to choose** liberty and eternal life, through the great Mediator of all men, or to choose captivity and death, according to the power and captivity of the devil ....[6]

Captivity is usually seen as a physical containment – prison, jail, being in an elevator when the power goes out, etc. But captivity in this scripture means that if we choose the enticements of the devil, we *give up our agency* forever. Being subject to Satan's reign means never again having agency, the freedom to choose. Prison from a different miserable angle.

> ... I would that ye should ... choose eternal life ... [a]nd not choose eternal death, according to the will of the flesh and the evil which is therein, which giveth the spirit of the devil power to captivate, to bring you down to hell, that he may reign over you in his own kingdom.[7]

Much as choosing carries with it responsibility and risks, the process is exciting. **Without the power to choose, life is dull.**

By the way, the young lady from Kazakhstan became quite adept at choosing menu items before she returned to her home country. And thoroughly enjoyed it.

☙

"Heavenly Father's goal in parenting
is not to have His children **do** what is right;
it is to have His children **choose to do** what is right
and ultimately become like Him."

– Dale G. Renlund

Chapter 8

Act
No One Eats Until Someone Takes a Risk

"Whatever you can do, or dream you can, begin it.
Boldness has genius, power and magic in it."
– Goethe

If we were never hungry, never thirsty, and if we were
impervious to heat and cold, would anything get done?

As we exercise agency,
we think, evaluate risks, and choose.

But agency is more than freedom to choose
and is not a passive gift.

It is a direct commandment to act,
exert effort, and achieve.

Action is the hinge-point of agency;
everything flows inescapably from it.

We will make mistakes, but
failures cannot be allowed to stop us.

Without taking risks and acting,
we will never progress.

Risk-free progress is impossible.

A successful lawyer wanted to buy a piece of land. His experience touched all components of the gift of agency. He had freedom to act, sufficient power, and an idea. He saw an opportunity, gave it much thought, collected the opinions of others, arranged financing, became confident, decided to act, and did so.

Then came the consequences. He was mocked, called stupid, and suffered derision from many. Approval seemed far off, if at all. But he persevered. Though he bought the land at a bargain price – 30 cents an acre in today's dollars – his exercise of risk and agency was called a folly. Seward's Folly.

Because he, William H. Seward, purchased … Alaska.

❧

Act, Do, Accomplish

Every morning in Africa, a gazelle wakes up. It knows it must run faster than the fastest lion or it will be killed. Every morning a lion wakes up. It knows it must run faster than the slowest gazelle or it will starve.

The moral of this well-worn story? Whether you're a lion or a gazelle, when the sun comes up, you'd better be running.

Scriptures instructing us to act are plentiful and direct:

God "gave unto man that he should **act** for himself."[1]

And we, being placed in a state to act, can do so "according to [our] wills and pleasures, whether to **do** evil or to **do** good …."[2] **Not be**; do.

That we "may **live and move and do** according to [our] own will …."[3]

Thou shalt **not be idle**; for he that is idle shall not eat the bread nor wear the garments of the laborer.[4]

That every man may **act** ... according to the **moral agency** which I have given unto him, that every man may be accountable for his own sins in the day of judgment.[5]

After thinking, assessing and choosing, we're finally at the nub of agency and can use our freedom and power to act, to do, to accomplish. We take risks and act.

Our First Risk

With agency's path of progress before us, we took our first risk when we decided to follow the Son of God and enter into mortality and come to a world where things will go wrong for our sake.

> Taking risks and acting means leaving your comfort zone.

Satan, on the other hand, played to those who feared risk and wanted reward without effort. They wanted a spiritual welfare state. He promised a risk-free return to God's presence though he knew he could not deliver. Satan's followers were afraid to be their own agents so they appointed the master deceiver to play that role. They gave up their gift. The biggest risk they took was not taking one at all, or so they thought.

When we chose to follow the Savior, we had no guarantee that we <u>would</u> return, only that we <u>could</u> return. The only guarantee we had is that Jesus Christ would overcome evil, conquer death, and provide a return path of grace and mercy to make up our shortfall. It would depend on us.

Teachers of Action

When Adam and Eve were given their eviction notice, the trees didn't go with them.

Previously all they had to do was pick whatever fruit they wanted (minus one) and their hunger was satisfied. But now they were commanded to earn their calories by the sweat of the brow. Seen by most of the world today as a punishment, it was actually a blessing – the

> "The soul's joy lies in doing."
>
> – Percy Shelley

blessing of effort that leads to progress. It was the beginning of the more robust agency that comes with the second act of our three-act play of life.

Consider the role of the lowly seed. Whereas seeds had produced the trees of Eden – walk-by restaurants, if you will – and no more effort required from our first parents than mere maintenance, now Adam and Eve had to start over and plant seeds in the lone and dreary mortal world. No more spontaneous production.

Perhaps the Lord prepared plants outside of Eden for Adam and Eve initially to harvest, but it wouldn't be as it was before. They would soon need to plant seeds, and before those seeds would produce edibles, they necessarily learned patience during hours of tilling, planting, cultivating, weeding, watering, and waiting.

Their first experiences with food-growing cycles had to be frustrating, but that in turn motivated them to learn planning, long-range preparation, and to be responsible for the results, good or bad. As hunger worked its powers, so did the elements, and these first mortals on earth soon needed shelter and warm clothes. More things requiring effort.

In the parable of the talents, the Savior endorsed the necessity of risk. Three servants were given stewardships of their master's money. When the master returned, two were rewarded because they took risks and increased the value of the talents they were given. The one who feared risk, who played it safe and buried the talent he was given, however, was chastised as a wicked and slothful servant.

We often hear the word *disaster* associated with the word *risk*. But there are also disasters from never taking a risk – the disasters of stagnation, of boredom, of self-hate, of unfulfilled lives, and the agony of "it could have been."

The bottom line: **Take prudent risks and act.**

Temptation

To progress and become what the Father wants us to become would be impossible without risks and temptations. If we are to be agents unto ourselves, we must be tempted.

> Wherefore, man could not act for himself save it should be that he was **enticed** by the one [being sweet] or the other [bitter].[6]

> And it must needs be that the devil should **tempt** the children of men, or they **could not be agents unto themselves**; for if they never should have bitter they could not know the sweet...[7]

Enticement comes in many forms. The most obvious is to be lured into doing outright evil – have an affair, rob a bank, view pornography, embezzle, take God's name in vain, ridicule believers … the list goes on. Or almost as insidious, in some cases more so, is the enticement to *procrastinate* and/or do nothing when given opportunities for righteous behaviors. This is the easiest one for Satan because it requires no action.

And then come enticements disguised as anti-enticements, particularly discouragement and ridicule: "You're not talented enough" or "No one's going to buy your poetry" or "Stay away from that wheelbarrow, Bubba, you don't know nuthin' about machinery."

If no temptation, then no opposition, no differing choices, no learning, no progress, no agency, and ... no existence.

> "Our doubts are traitors and make us lose the good we oft might win by fearing to attempt."
>
> – Shakespeare

Freeze

When it comes to positive works with reasonable risks, Satan hopes we won't even try to act. He works to curtail our freedom, confuse our thinking, muddle our choices, and now tries to freeze us from acting, from experimenting, from doing. His motto: "Don't just do something; stand there."

One tactic is to confuse non-action with patience. Yes, there is a time for patience, for thought and reflection whether our decision to act is the right one, but too much patience leads to procrastination and then rigidity. The tool is *lull*.

> And others will he pacify, and lull them away into carnal security, that they will say: All is well in Zion; yea, Zion prospereth ... and thus the devil cheateth their souls, and leadeth them carefully down to hell.[8]

After All is Said, But Not Yet Done ... Act

We often hear the term "**exercise** agency." Love the verb. Like a muscle, we use it or lose it. Agency is not a passive pronouncement, but a direct **commandment to act**, do something, achieve, accomplish. Otherwise there can be no experience, no progress, no life.

Thoughts are necessary forerunners to action. If we think good thoughts, we will acquire a desire to do good things, and vice versa.

"In essence, **knowledge is an intellectual understanding** of truth," explained Elder Tad R. Callister, "while **faith is a principle of action** – it motivates us to live what we believe."[9]

> Faith without verbs is dead.

Hurricane Harvey in August 2017 caused over 100 deaths and $125 billion in damages, tied with Hurricane Katrina in 2005 as the costliest hurricane in American history.[10] Of the many acts of kindness and courage it spawned, the initiative of residents and concerned people from hundreds of miles around was especially noteworthy. As the winds subsided, the waters didn't and many were trapped. Boat owners formed a rescue flotilla with boats usually used for water-skiing and fishing – "an unprecedented do-it-yourself relief effort that came to define Hurricane Harvey."[11] No instigation from government. Totally private initiative. Wonderful results as thousands of people were taken to dry land. Agency and **action** as the Lord intended.

A similar exercise of agency happened when the Teton Dam in Idaho ruptured in 1976 flooding several downstream communities. By the time government agencies arrived with bologna sandwiches, they were met by Relief Society sisters serving hot casseroles. **Initiative** – doing things for the good of others without being told.

Winston Churchill wasn't hesitant about many things. But when he took his first art lesson, he gingerly placed a dob of paint on the canvas. His art instructor grabbed the brush, sopped up a goodly amount of the goop, and splashed a bold swath of it across the canvas. His advice to Sir Winston: Don't be afraid of the canvas. **Begin**.

Yoda said, "There is no try; only do." That is true when "try" is half-hearted or an excuse for not giving it your all. In the sense of experiment, jump in whole heartedly and test things out. Did Edison "do" a light-bulb? Yes, but he did many **tries** before the "done."

> **Agency** and **agenda** come from the same root. If you have the former, create the latter.

French aristocrat Marquis de Lafayette could have coasted for life on the wealth of his distinguished landowning family, but sought action in the budding American Revolution in 1777, volunteering to serve without pay. And action again in the French Revolution of 1789. And the July Revolution of 1830.[12] **Seek the new**; seek adventure.

If curiosity can be defined by the number of one's interests, then the most curious person in history would be Leonardo da Vinci. Among his interests, each at which he invariably excelled, were "invention, painting, sculpting, architecture, science, music, mathematics, engineering, literature, anatomy, geology, astronomy, botany, writing, history, and cartography."[13] **Wonder** about everything; follow your curiosity.

Mozart was a restless, prodigious genius. He composed over 600 works – from symphonies to sonatas, concertos to operas – in his short 35 years of life. His own assessment: "Believe me, I do not like idleness, but **work**."

Although his ruthless methods are not to be applauded, Peter the Great, Tsar of Russia, "led a cultural revolution that replaced some of the traditionalist and medieval social and political systems with ones that were modern, scientific, Westernized, and based on the Enlightenment."[14] He **changed** things.

To break a board with his bare hand, the karate expert does not aim *at* the board, but at a point in space a few inches *below* it. In the process of reaching the extended goal, the original objective is achieved as a byproduct. Set extended **goals**.

Alma spoke to Zoramites of lower socio-economic status and suggested the same theme: try an experiment by planting a seed in your heart and see what happens. **Try it**, you'll like it.

President Russell M. Nelson on September 15, 2018: "We are living in the most crucial era in the history of the world. Since the beginning of time, prophets have foreseen our day and prophesied about what would take place during this winding-up period before the Savior comes again. As a church, **we need to be <u>doing</u> what the Savior wishes us to <u>do</u>**. And as a people we need to be looking and acting like true followers of Jesus Christ."[15]

❧

What would have happened if Joseph Smith wondered for
the rest of his life which church was true, but never
went into a secluded grove to pray about it?

Chapter 9

Opposition
The Wonderful World of Friction

"Opposition permits us to grow toward what our
Heavenly Father would have us become."
— Dallin H. Oaks

From gentle friction to hostile enemy, of necessity for
our progress there must be opposition in all things.

This world was created
so things would go wrong.

As things move from an ordered
to a disordered state (entropy),
effort is necessary.

But man does not act
save he be enticed by opposites.

As he acts, there must be friction
or there is no movement.

Similarly, without resistance,
nothing is strengthened; without
contrast, there is no persuasion.

Agency requires opposition,
without which there can be
no progress, no exaltation.

Without opposition,
all is a compound in one
and nothing exists.

About 15 years after World War II, I began knocking on doors in Germany seeking people who might be interested in hearing about the re-established original Christian church. Although Germany was full throttle cleaning up rubble and rebuilding society (its famous *Wirtschaftswunder*, economic miracle), memories of war were hard to erase.

How often we heard the complaint: "If God existed, He wouldn't have let these things happen." It was more than a convenient excuse to turn down our offer to explain our beliefs; many felt it deeply.

Such thinking may seem reasonable for those who don't understand the fullness of agency, those who think agency only means freedom. They enjoy their own freedoms but feel that a just God would intervene immediately to prevent others from using their freedoms if such acts hurt innocent people, especially if on a massive scale. Therefore evil justifies atheism.

They don't get it. They may mouth the words good and evil, but don't appreciate that in this world there would be **no progress toward the good without evil to push against**.

*
*

Opposition Is a Continuum

At one end of the scale, friction is necessary or there can be no progress. At the other end, it is overwhelming opposition that disrupts and blocks the plan of progress.

Our job is to *use* good friction to our advantage and *fight* it when it isn't. But if friction lessens to the point of disappearing, a frictionless environment produces nothing and can never toughen one for the challenges of life.

President Dallin H. Oaks:

"To be meaningful, mortal choices had to be made between contesting forces of good and evil. There had to be opposition and, therefore, an adversary, who was cast out because of rebellion and was allowed to tempt God's children to act contrary to God's plan."[1]

The Nothing

One of the simplest yet most profound explanations in the scriptures is the great statement by Lehi to Jacob "that there is an opposition in all things." But do we pay enough attention to what he then said? That if there is no opposition, then "all things must needs be a **compound in one**; wherefore, if it should be one body it must needs remain as dead, having no life neither death..." Now, with this "compound in one" being dead, Lehi hammers home his point that there is no life as we know it with its pluses and minuses – no life, death, corruption, incorruption, happiness, misery, sense, insensibility.[2] How fun is that?

> "Adversity, if handled correctly, can be a blessing in our lives."
>
> – Joseph B. Wirthlin

Nuuuh-thiiing.

In fact, as he continues, it is so nothing that it "destroy[s] the wisdom of God and his eternal purposes." And what are those purposes? The eternal progress and exaltation of His children. Further, this lack of opposition would destroy "also the power, and the mercy, and the justice of God."[3]

Then the elaboration:

If there is no law, there is no sin

If no sin, no righteousness

If no righteousness, no happiness

If no righteousness nor happiness,
no punishment nor misery

If these things are not,
there is no God

If no God, then we are not,
neither the earth

No creation of things,
neither to act nor to be acted upon

Wherefore, all things
must have vanished away.[4]

A more powerful logic chain would be difficult to find in all of man's philosophies.

It reminds me of "The NeverEnding Story," a children's tale in which the villain is The Nothing. From a review: "In the movie, the Nothing is described as a tremendous, destructive storm, covering the sky with dark clouds, winds and lightning. In the novel however, it is stated to be a formless, featureless negation of existence impossible to describe, surrounded by an overworldly mist that engulfs everything around."[5]

A "formless, featureless negation of existence." A pretty good description of Lehi's explanation of a world without opposition in all things.

Temptation, Misery, Pain

Let's continue with Lehi's beautiful expansions on opposition and its meanings. First, in an environment of opposition where God has created "things to act and things to be acted upon," man has the agency to choose and do. But there can be no action until there are enticements, as discussed earlier, playing a role to bring about God's purposes for us, as detailed in 2 Nephi 2:14-27:

> And to bring about his eternal purposes, ... it must needs be that there was an **opposition**; even the forbidden fruit in opposition to the tree of life; the one being sweet and the other bitter. Wherefore, the Lord God gave unto man that he should **act for himself**. Wherefore, man could not act for himself save it should be that he was **enticed** by the one or the other.

Enter stage left Satan and his misery:

> [An] angel ... had fallen from heaven [and] became a devil, having sought that which was evil before God. And [having] become miserable forever, he sought also the **misery** of all mankind.

Adam and Eve partook of the forbidden fruit, were kicked out of the garden, and our days have been prolonged so we have time to repent while in this state of probation. The plot thickens:

> [If] Adam had not transgressed ... he would have remained in the garden of Eden. And all things which were created must have **remained in the same state** in which they were after they were created; and they must have remained forever, and had no end.

Interminable boredom.

[They] would have had no children ... remained in a state of innocence, **having no joy, for they knew no misery**; doing no good, for they knew no sin.

But it was all in the plan:

But behold, all things have been done in the wisdom of him who knoweth all things.

And here the famous verse:

Adam fell that men might be; and **men are that they might have joy**.[6]

Perhaps we could fill in the role of agency this way:

Through Adam, men fell that they might exercise agency, or have agency of others acted upon them, that they might experience misery that they might have joy.

Similarly:

... and they taste the bitter, that they may know to prize the good.

Lehi's elaboration on agency through the atonement of the Messiah could not be clearer than in these two verses:

And the Messiah cometh in the fulness of time, that he may redeem the children of men from the fall. And because that they are redeemed from the fall they have become **free forever**, knowing good from evil; to **act for themselves and not to be acted upon** ....

And they are **free to choose liberty and eternal life**, through the great Mediator of all men, **or to choose captivity and death**, according to the captivity and power of the devil ....

Entropy, Ice, and Thumbs

Forward to today's time and three everyday examples of opposition:

- The law of entropy states that all things in nature move from an ordered to a disordered state. In other words, the world was created so things would go wrong. Rivers erode land, wood crumbles, food rots, and even sour cream goes sour. The greater the disorder, the more friction presents itself, and the more effort is required to overcome that deterioration. The wonderful world of friction.

- Ever traveled in snow country in the winter? Ever driven on black ice? If so, you know the frustration when your tires fail to "grab" enough to move the car forward. When scientists measure slipperiness, what they call the coefficient of friction, if it's ever zero, pal, you're not going to move. Thank goodness for tire chains.

- The first and second fingers on your hand are not exactly tweezers. Ever try to pick up a small object using just those two digits? Each finger works better when it is paired with the thumb – the "opposing" element. Only then can the human hand gain enough purchase to perform its many tasks. Another example of opposition that helps us.

> You never run out of things that can go wrong. That's the fun of life.

It's in every facet of our lives. No opposition, no friction, nothing to push against ... no progress.

One other thing – Satan actually facilitates the Father's plan. "So it is," explains President Dallin H. Oaks, "that the evil one, who opposed and sought to *destroy* the Father's plan, actually *facilitated* it, because it is opposition that enables choice and it is the opportunity of making the right choices that leads to the growth that is the purpose of the Father's plan."[7] [Emphasis in original]

Talk about unintended consequences the adversary didn't anticipate. But just as the Savior knew what He was doing when He chose Judas, so the Father knew Lucifer.

Tribulations and Comfort

Pain is a powerful professor. It is the process through which we pay attention and learn.

Considering the afflictions of life – the failures, injuries, pain, disappointments, destructions, difficulties, wars, malignancies, mold, and mosquitoes – it's amazing how many scriptures speak to such tribulations and assure us they are reasons … to be **happy**, they are causes for **hope**.

First, the inevitability of and reasons for tribulation:

… for it must needs be that offences come …[8] … that we must through much tribulation enter into the kingdom of God."[9] Many are the afflictions of the righteous …[10] I have refined thee, I have chosen thee in the furnace of affliction.[11] … and all things wherewith you have been afflicted shall work together for your good …."[12]

We need the bitter to know the sweet, and then come the blessings:

… he shall **consecrate thine afflictions** for thy gain.[13] … blessed is … he that is faithful in tribulation …. Ye cannot behold with your natural eyes … the glory which shall follow after much tribulation. For after much tribulation come the blessings.[14]

Sweet are the uses of adversity, as Shakespeare said.

We can especially take heart from D&C 122. Here the Prophet Joseph is languishing in Liberty Jail (talk about an oxymoron) and receives comfort from the Lord beginning with a recitation of umpteen situations of "if this" and "if that" nature that are as encompassing and overwhelming as can be. To wit …

> … false brethren, perils among robbers, false accusations, tear thee from family, dragged to prison, cast into hands of murderers, sentenced to death, cast into the ocean, very jaws of hell gape open after thee …

Then the simple assurance: "… all these things shall give thee experience and shall be **for thy good**."

In this same tone, a few sayings from latter-day leaders:

> President Gordon B. Hinckley: "Give us faith to smile through our tears, knowing it is all part of the eternal plan."

> President Thomas S. Monson: "Only the Master knows the depths of our trials. He alone offers us eternal peace in that time of adversity. He alone touches our tortured souls."

> Elder Joseph B. Wirthlin: "I know why there must be opposition in all things. Adversity, if handled correctly, can be a blessing in our lives. We can learn to love it."

> Elder Orson F. Whitney: "No pain that we suffer, no trial that we experience is wasted. … All that we suffer and all that we endure … builds up our characters, purifies our hearts, expands our souls, and makes us more tender and charitable … and it is through sorrow and suffering, toil and tribulation, that we gain the education that we come here to acquire …."[15]

If we appreciate opposition in all things, if we exercise our agency to the fullest, we will have happiness in this life no matter the tribulations. God will balance the scales. In due and proper time, all negative experiences will redound to our good.

"At times," explained President M. Russell Ballard, "we will be affected adversely by the way other people choose to exercise their agency. Our Heavenly Father feels so strongly about protecting our agency that **he allows his children to exercise it, either for good or for evil**."[16]

The Apostle Paul said of the seeming unfairness, "I am exceeding joyful in all our tribulation."[17]

And the purpose of it all was succinctly stated by President Henry B. Eyring: "Opposition will strengthen our faith in Jesus Christ, as it has since the days of the prophet Joseph Smith."[18]

❧

The ultimate comforting thought is that we will never be called upon to suffer more "pains and afflictions and temptations of every kind"[19] than the Savior in our behalf.

In the world ye shall have tribulation:
But be of good cheer; I have overcome the world.[20]

Chapter 10

Creativity
Beauty and the Feast

"Where the spirit does not work with the hand
there is no art."
— Leonardo da Vinci

Those who have glimpsed the hereafter in near-death experiences uniformly describe a place of unimaginably beautiful light and colors, music and love. The creativity of robust agency here enhances the aesthetic in this world and prepares us for the next.

The stronger the agency,
the greater the freedom to
explore and compare.

More comparisons
produce more connections
and thus new thoughts.

Thoughts in turn trigger emotions.

There are no new emotions,
but thoughts to which emotions
are attached are infinite.

Thought-emotion pairings
produce images.

The more such pairings,
the greater the variety of
sight, sound, and written images.

The deeper and more intense
the images, the greater the beauty
and more sublime the product.

Creativity in art, music, literature.

H ave you ever heard of Harmenszoon van Rijn?

A child of the early 1600s, he led a roller-coaster life – the whole gamut from spectacular success, wealth and fame to financial collapse, bankruptcy and poverty, and the deaths of three children. He mingled with royalty and the elite of his day, but also had a lifelong habit of studying beggars and the homeless.[1] How could such a scope of emotions and observations of others not influence his creative process?

It did. The world knows him by one name only … Rembrandt.

⌘

If Napoleon had not invaded Russia,
would Tchaikovsky still have written the 1812 Overture?

Brain and Heart

We carry all emotions within us, in varying degrees, and they are brought to the surface by stimuli of the moment. A gunshot, for example, may trigger fear; name-calling may cause anger; a full moon, romance. As thoughts activate emotions and emotions intensify thoughts, brain and heart work together and we **feel our thoughts**. The higher the intensity of this feeling, the longer the thought will be remembered and tinkered with.

Musicians and artists of all stripes are known for their deeper, intense emotions and their ability to remember. Thus thought-emotion pairings do more than seep into and infuse their work; they become their work as put to paper, paint, and the vibrations we call music.

One expert maintains that images and memories "pass colorfully and plastically through the souls of the artists" and the "early awakening of strong emotions in childhood is proven among many composers." Further:

[An artist] "without extreme strength of memory for such recollections is just as unthinkable as the artist without an imagination that is capable of employing such recollections in **new associations**. … In the [ever-active] fantasy of the musician, emotions are preserved with the most **minute gradations** of color and rhythm."[2]

If new associations are the essence of *creativity*, then the variety of color and rhythm gradations are the essence of *beauty*.

Naturally, we see positive emotions more often with robust agency because of freedom and power to act, and we appreciate a Mozart known for his playful mood, jokes and puns. But adversity with its negative emotions can also generate creativity as one struggles with opposition, friction being a necessary component of agency and progress. Beethoven, for example, was grave and sullen, a bi-polar introvert and gloomy as a child. Many of his works reflect those emotions, but others, such as his Ninth Symphony, are joyful and triumphant. His Egmont Overture is both – brooding and somber for ten of its eleven minutes and then in the final minute becomes one of the best examples of triumphal music.

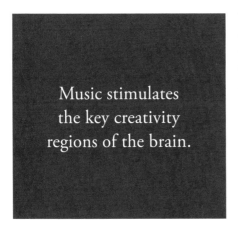

Music stimulates the key creativity regions of the brain.

So who are these geniuses who give us so much refinement and enjoyment? How do they describe themselves and their creative processes?

Geniuses Tell Us Who They Are

"Music is my life and my life is music." – Mozart

"The most original of authors are not so because they advance what is new, but more because they know how to say something, as if it had <u>never been said before</u>." – Goethe

"I was made to <u>work</u>. If you are equally industrious, you will be equally successful." – Bach

"I <u>think</u>; therefore I am." – Descartes

"I am one of those who will go on <u>doing</u> till all doings are at an end." – Mozart

"The emotions are sometimes so strong that I <u>work without knowing it</u>. The strokes come like speech." – Van Gogh

"I must lose myself in <u>action</u>, lest I wither in despair." – Tennyson

"Rembrandt goes so <u>deep</u> into the mysterious that he says things for which there are no words in any language." – Van Gogh

"I seem to have been only like a boy … finding a smoother pebble or a prettier shell than ordinary whilst the <u>great ocean of truth</u> lay all undiscovered." – Newton

Geniuses Tell Us How They Do It

"I <u>saw</u> the angel in the marble and I carved until I set him free." – Michelangelo

"I was never a quick writer, but composed with great <u>care and efforts</u>." – Haydn

"Every artist dips his brush into his own soul, and paints <u>his own nature</u> into his pictures." – Beecher

"I have not failed. I've just found 10,000 ways that won't work." – Edison

"To begin, <u>begin</u>." – Wordsworth

"Let him that would move the world, first <u>move himself</u>." – Socrates

"Constancy. Not he who begins, but he who <u>perseveres</u>." – Da Vinci

"If any man wish to write in a clear style, let him be first <u>clear in his thoughts</u>; and if any would write in a noble style, let first possess a <u>noble soul</u>." – Goethe

"<u>Passion</u> is the genesis of genius." – Galileo

"The secret of genius is to carry the <u>spirit of the child</u> into old age, which means never losing your <u>enthusiasm</u>." – Huxley

"Every obstacle yields to stern <u>resolve</u>." – Da Vinci

"If you hear a voice within you say 'you cannot paint,' then by all means paint, and that voice will be silenced." – Van Gogh

"Genius is <u>patience</u>." – Newton

"Do not be like the cat who wanted a fish but was afraid to get his paws wet." – Shakespeare

"Iron rusts from disuse, stagnant water loses its purity, and in cold weather becomes frozen: even so does inaction sap the vigors of the mind." – Da Vinci

"People err who think my art comes easily to me. I assure you, dear friend, nobody has devoted so much <u>time and thought</u> to compositions as I." – Mozart

Geniuses Recognize Genius

"The aim and final end of all music should be none other than the glory of God and the refreshment of the soul." – Bach

"When I think upon my God, my heart is full of joy that the notes dance and leap from my pen." – Haydn

"I play the notes as they are written, but it is God who makes the music." – Bach

"Whether I was in my body or out of my body as I wrote it I know not. God knows." – Händel, on writing *Messiah*

"I do not feel obliged to believe that the same God who has endowed us with sense, reason, and intellect has intended us to forgo their use." – Galileo

"When I admire the wonders of a sunset or the beauty of the moon, my soul expands in the worship of the creator." – Gandhi

Geniuses View the World

"Love of beauty is taste. The creation of beauty is art." – Emerson

"The object of art is to give life a shape." – Shakespeare

"The chief function of the body is to carry the brain around." – Edison

"Everything has beauty, but not everyone sees it." – Confucius

"Music … will help dissolve your perplexities and purify your character and sensibilities, and in time of care and sorrow, will keep a fountain of joy alive in you." – Bonhoeffer

"A thing of beauty is a joy forever." – Keats

"A creation of importance can only be produced when its author isolates himself; it is a child of solitude." – Goethe

Visualize

Geniuses have three traits the average person has yet to develop (yes, genius-ness can be learned):

- They have more **complex neuron networks**, the result of having made more comparisons and establishing more connections than others.

- They have trained themselves to **play "what if"** – to turn things upside down, this way and that, to see a situation from various angles, not just the order the stimuli were presented.

- They have developed the **patience** to bounce new thoughts against more of these networks than the average person. They give them equal weight.

Although geniuses look at the same things and experience the same initial stimuli as anyone else, their talent is the ability to "see" connections most miss. But if no one sees what can be, creativity and the improvement we call refinement will never be.

Mozart, who this day certainly continues his craft, left us this great glimpse of music in heaven before going there:

> "I have never written the music that was in my heart to write; perhaps I never shall with this brain and these fingers, but I know that hereafter it will be written; when instead of these few inlets of the senses through which we now secure impressions from without, there shall be a **flood of impressions** from all sides; and instead of these few tones of our little octave, there shall be an **infinite scale of harmonies** – for I feel it – I am sure of it. This world of music, whose borders even now I have scarcely entered, is a reality, is immortal."[3]

℘

So to the original question: If Napoleon had not invaded Russia, would Tchaikovsky still have written the 1812 Overture? I believe he would. It may have appeared in a slightly different form, but that music was in him.

It only would have required a different grain of Russian-history sand in his oyster.

Chapter 11

Innovation
Applied Creativity

"Most of my ideas first belonged to people
who did not bother to develop them."
– Thomas Edison

Innovation destroys jobs … and creates more and better ones.

The stronger the agency,
the greater the freedom
and thus creativity.

The greater the creativity,
the more opportunities to apply it.

Applied creativity produces
innovations and inventions.

Successful innovations
encourage further creativity.

The more numerous
and creative the innovations,
the higher the standard of living.

In 1894, strict vegetarians John and Will were looking for new meatless meals to feed patients at their sanitarium. One day they forgot about the mush they were cooking and the wheat berries became stale. Being frugal, they didn't want to toss it out so they ran it through rollers hoping to create a dough. They got crumbles instead – flakes. So they roasted them. A hit.

Then their dendrites and neurons kicked in: might there be other grains, they asked themselves, that would flake and could be roasted and used as a breakfast food? In due time, they experimented with kernels of corn. The result: cornflakes. Invented by the Kellogg brothers in Battle Creek, Michigan.

ɕↄ

Innovation is the application of creativity. It's the excitement of discovery as we tinker, experiment, and perhaps invent – the thrill of exploring the complexities of life. You find innovation or it finds you.

Let's look at four types: dissatisfaction, serendipity, curiosity, and momentum.

Dissatisfaction – Horses and Autos

Setting: You have a need and you search for a solution.

To Henry Ford is attributed the saying, "If I had asked people what they wanted, they would have said faster horses." Dissatisfaction with the top speed of horses led to the invention of the automobile, the price of which came down thanks to Ford's invention of the assembly line (itself a dissatisfaction with previous methods), thus disproving the New York Times 1902 prediction that cars would never catch on because "the prices will never be sufficiently low."[1]

A grouchy customer, complaining of soggy fried potatoes, prodded one chef to slice them as thinly as possible, which produced the immediately popular potato chip courtesy of George Crum, Saratoga Springs, NY, 1853.[2]

Needs lead to inventions. Even picky little needs such as how to mark the pages of the hymns your church choir is going to sing next Sunday. Arthur Fry, a 3M employee was aware of a not-so-sticky adhesive discovered by a fellow employee. Mr. Need meet Mr. Solution. Thus the creation of Post-It notes in 1974, known in today's vernacular as stick-ums.

> "The key to economic prosperity is the *organized creation of dissatisfaction.*"
>
> – Charles Kettering

Dissatisfaction applies to services as well as products. Fred Smith was dissatisfied with the speed that products, especially from the burgeoning computer industry, could be delivered. He dreamed of an overnight delivery service, but the giants in the industry, the U.S. Postal Service and UPS, still thought in terms of point-to-point – producer to consumer – deliveries. So if a system has 100 markets, for example, that means 9900 direct delivery routes. Cumbersome and slow.

Smith asked himself, "How do other things move?" and realized that information and money move through a hub-and-spoke method, significantly more efficient than direct delivery. If it works for information and bank clearinghouses, he thought, why not for products? So using both airplanes and trucks (the combination hadn't been tried before), he developed … Federal Express.[3]

And it didn't take long for a jealous UPS to follow suit.

Creativity and innovation are mutually encouraging. One can become excited about discovering new insights if he knows he has the freedom to tinker and apply the results of his creative thinking – especially if he feels restless or less than satisfied with the status quo.

Serendipity – From Penicillin to Microwaves

Setting: You notice something unusual and pursue the reason.

Bacteriological researcher Alexander Fleming left a petri dish of staphylococcus bacteria uncovered while he went on vacation. Upon returning, he noticed a mold on the culture had killed most of the bacteria. "I didn't plan to revolutionize all medicine by discovering the world's first antibiotic, or bacteria killer. But I guess that was exactly what I did." Penicillin, 1928.

A Raytheon Corporation employee was working on a new type of vacuum tube when he noticed a candy bar in his pocket had begun to melt. Hmmm. What kind of power is going on? So he tried kernels of corn. When they popped, he knew he was on to something. Ray Spencer, 1945, father of the microwave oven.

Wilhelm Röntgen was tinkering "when he noticed that a piece of paper covered in barium platinocyanide began to glow across the room." He knew that rays from his cathode emitter wouldn't travel that far.

> "If necessity is the mother of invention, then dissatisfaction must be its father."
>
> – Jeffrey Fry

Had to be another kind but he didn't know what to call them. So they became… X-rays.[4]

Constantin Fahlberg, a Russian chemist working for a Baltimore firm in 1878, failed to wash his hands upon leaving his lab one evening. He sat down for dinner, "picked up a roll with his hand and bit into a remarkably sweet crust." Remembering that he had spilled an experimental compound over his hands earlier that day, he ran back to the lab "where he tasted everything on his worktable" until he found the source – three chemicals had reacted to produce benzoic sulfimide. Saccharin, 300 times sweeter than sugar.[5]

Curiosity – Self-Cleaning Ovens

Setting: You get an idea and tie it to someone else's need.

As improvements were made to stoves and ovens over the years, guidance was solicited from American housewives. Asked what they wanted, women in the focus groups suggested re-arranging lights, buttons, knobs, and hot plates, but no one ever said she wanted a self-cleaning oven. When engineers at General Electric, following their curiosity to innovate, produced precisely that in 1963, the acceptance was enthusiastic and the rest is history. People didn't know what they needed until it was put in front of them. A now-standard feature was innovated into existence without a known demand prodding it.

> "Disruptive technologies typically enable new markets to emerge."
>
> – Clayton Christensen

Similar situation with James Watt. Studying instruments and working with steam engines at the University of Glasgow, he realized that existing models "wasted energy by repeatedly cooling and reheating the cylinder." To solve this he introduced a simple but significant improvement on the design – a separate condenser. Ergo, the first practical steam engine and a driving force of the industrial revolution, 1781.[6]

Momentum – Clock Gears to Computers

The idea: Build on someone else's innovation.

It began with the mechanical clocks of the 13th and 14th centuries. Teeth on the edge of rotating gear wheels pushed counterpart gear teeth to orchestrate the movement of clock hands. Metal touching metal.

Then came the music box in the 1500s. A pegged cylinder would rotate and little nubs of metal sticking out – the pegs – would pluck the tuned teeth in a steel comb in the box to produce music. Fortunately, someone soon invented removable cylinders so it wouldn't be the same tune over and over. Player pianos followed the same idea but had to wait two centuries for one more innovation to be perfected.

That big change came courtesy of a weaving company in Lyon, France beginning in 1725 and a final breakthrough into an automated weaving loom in 1804. In place of nubs, gear teeth and pegs … a hole. Holes in paper or cards controlled which threads were woven into a fabric in what order. A punched card would rotate over a box and slender rods would go through holes signaling the underlying weave mechanisms which thread to shuttle to the other end of the fabric. Next card, next thread. Warp and woof.[7]

> "Economic cycles are natural. Cultural cycles are often imposed by government. Independent innovation changes the trajectory of both."
>
> – Marc Nuttle

Then came the key innovation in the infant computer industry. Instead of placing rods through holes to instruct an underlying mechanism, use a light or an electrical signal. Thus was born the stiff-paper punch card – the set of instructions read to a computer one line of code per card. And pity the poor user who trips and scatters hundreds of punch cards. (I know.)

Now we have digital inputs – no teeth or pegs, no holes and rods, not even any tangible material through which light or electrical signals pass. Straight digital input whether direct or scanned.

And who knows what's next? The point is, each innovation builds on a past innovation and spawns another in the future. God's plan for **inspiration unfolds line upon line**, to borrow a familiar phrase, to those who innovate.

Creative Destruction

Look again at the above examples of innovation. Each one, without exception, destroyed jobs. No dedicated facilities today manufacture buggy whips, horse-drawn carriages, music box cylinders, telegraphs, 45 rpm vinyl records, typewriters, reel-to-reel tape recorders, computer punch cards, etc., the list goes on and on. In each case, people suffered loss of a job, loss of income.

But out of the destruction – this creative destruction – come even more jobs and even better jobs … if someone is willing to **up his game**. Innovate or evaporate.

The problem arises when a third party, such as government, gets involved to protect special interests under the guise of "saving jobs" and "relieving suffering." They know transitions from good to better will always cause displacements, even hunger. But capitalizing on short-term adjustments is too tempting for those seeking power and gain. Further, government bureaucracies emphasize alignment and conformity, antithetical to the spirit of innovation. In almost all cases, job protection hinders progress.

ᥱᖚ

The first dictionary definition for *innovate* is to "try out new ideas." The listed synonyms are *revolutionize, invent, modernize, originate*, and *transform*. Each one suggests we **change the status quo, improve, do things differently**.

In short, progress … both verb and noun.

Chapter 12

Prosperity
Fruits of Agency and a Free Market

"The most important single central fact
about a free market is that no exchange takes place
unless both parties benefit."
– Milton Friedman

Agency with its creativity and innovations produces entrepreneurs
who improve the quality of life and financial well-being of more
people than any other concept or system in the world.

Agency includes the right to take risks
and be rewarded or punished.

The greater the agency and freedom, the greater
the confidence effort will not go unrewarded.

Such confidence creates opportunities
to tinker and innovate thus leading to
inventions of products and services.

Tinkerers and risk-takers become
the entrepreneurs who improve our
quality of life and financial well-being.

Tinker innovation flourishes where there is
economic freedom to offer one's skills, labor,
and inventions to the highest bidder.

As agency is honored and entrepreneurs
take risks and act, a free market unfolds
and produces competitive cooperation.

If competition is based on merits,
not government favoritism, the ensuing
cooperation enhances prosperity.

If people are starving, look for
political failures, not agricultural.

The free-market system unlocks
inventiveness of the people.

Agency – the big bang creation
of free-market economies.

Born in a one-room cottage in Scotland, he emigrated to America with his extremely poor parents at age 13. Working from dawn to dusk hauling spindles of cotton to workers at the looms for $1.20 a week, he became determined to do better. Obviously referring to himself, he later described the emigrant as "the capable, energetic, ambitious, **discontented** man."

His discontent pushed him to heed agency's command to act.

And act he did. Bobbin boy, messenger, telegraph operator, and then a superintendent at Pennsylvania Railroad at age 24. Along the way he became a *voracious reader*, basically his own teacher, and began investing. By age 30, he was involved in businesses ranging from iron works to railroads to oil wells. He subsequently created the largest steel manufacturing company in the world.

The poor immigrant boy from Scotland is now known as one of the richest men in history, a net worth of over $300 billion in today's dollars. He then spent the rest of his life contributing huge sums to many causes, best known of which were his gifts to build free public libraries. He once wrote: "To try to make the world in some way better than you found it is to have a noble motive in life."[1]

Prosperity properly applied.

Andrew Carnegie.

❧

The Key to Prosperity

Prosperity as the reward for keeping the commandments was spoken to Lehi by the Lord and emphasized five additional times in the Book of Mormon:[2]

> Inasmuch as ye shall keep my commandments ye shall prosper in the land; but inasmuch as you will not keep my commandments ye shall be cut off from my presence.

From the way this promise begins, we expect a simple parallel:

Keep commandments → Prosper

Not keep commandments → Not prosper

But the final phrase is an unexpected twist. Instead of a parallel – "not prosper in the land" – we get "cut off from my presence." Three things come to mind:

1. Being cut off from the Lord's presence is significantly more serious than not prospering on earth.

2. If you do not keep commandments you could still possibly prosper, but you may not dwell in God's presence.

3. The reverse doesn't hold: Just because you prosper doesn't necessarily mean you've kept the commandments.

The key point is that keeping the commandments can bring prosperity here and the blessing of living in God's presence hereafter.

> And the Lord did visit them and prosper them, and they became a large and wealthy people.[3]

Agency's Dual Role

As noted before, agency is both a gift and a commandment. **It is the gift to run one's own life and it is the commandment to act.**

God can directly bless those who live the gospel, but more often He sets up a natural mechanism which, if followed, leads to the blessing.

Consider this chain:

Prosperity begins as we accurately assess
a situation before choosing and acting.

Accurate assessment requires mental clarity.

Those who live the commandments have
cleaner minds than those who do not. They are
less plagued with improper neuron connections.

A clean, less-cluttered mind is a more
intelligent mind and allows more light on a topic,
intelligence and light being synonymous.

More intelligence by definition means
better connections and better ideas.

Better ideas in turn lead to better innovation,
more and better products, more wealth,
better health – prosperity.

On our path to prosperity, we find light, intelligence, creativity, and freedom intertwined. When people respect the agency and sovereignty of one another, tremendous energy and light and creativity are released benefiting not only the individual but also everyone in that society. As this light multiplies on itself, we have the very definition of eternal progress:

> That which is of God is light; and he that receiveth light, and continueth in God, receiveth more light; and that light growth brighter and brighter until the perfect day.[4]

Conditions on the Ground

For innovative ideas to move from mind to actuality, the right conditions must prevail. **The foundation for prosperity includes the right to own private property, a sound currency, the rule of law, and the sacredness of contracts.**[5] When these are in place, we have the freedom and ingenuity of the free-market system – willing sellers and willing buyers. And if this free willingness applies universally to products, services, or one's time, it is astonishing how much the system will improve the lives of everyone.

> "America's economic exceptionalism has been the product of freedom and opportunity, secured through limited government."[6]

To preserve this free-market prosperity, government's only roles should be to (1) create a sound medium of exchange, (2) establish a modicum of basic law that protects property, and (3) guarantee inviolate contracts willingly entered into. If it ever establishes wage and price controls – telling people what they can charge and what they can earn – say goodbye to the most productive system ever devised.

"The record of history is absolutely crystal clear," said Milton Friedman, "that there is no alternative way so far discovered of improving the lot of the ordinary people that can hold a candle to the **productive activities that are unleashed by the free-enterprise system**."

While we're at it, three more quotes from this great economist:[7]

"The only way that has ever been discovered to have a lot of people cooperate together voluntarily is through the free market. And that's why it's so essential to preserve individual freedom."

"I think that nothing is so important for freedom as recognizing in the law each individual's natural right to property, and giving individuals a sense that they **own something that they're responsible for**, that they have control over, and that they can dispose of."

"A major source of objection to a free economy is precisely that it … gives people what they want instead of what a particular group thinks they ought to want. Underlying most arguments against the free market is a lack of belief in freedom itself."

How anyone cannot believe in the power and rightness of a free-market system – willing sellers and willing buyers – is beyond me. The evidence is abundant. Choose any product and trace what it cost in labor hours to purchase when it was first available compared to today.

- An automobile in 1908 cost 4700 hours; it now costs less than 1500.
- A refrigerator in 1915 cost 3200 hours; it now costs less than 70.
- Color TV in 1954 cost 560 hours; now less than 25.
- A cellphone in 1984 cost 450 hours; it now costs less than 10.[8]

The slide in hours spent per value gained cannot be attributed to government regulations, wage and price controls, or central planning. It's the free market in action, with government playing only its role of protecting property.

Property as Agency Motivator

From the 134th section of the Doctrine and Covenants:

> We believe that no government can exist in peace, except such laws are framed and held inviolate as will secure to each individual the free exercise of conscience, **the right and control of property**, and the protection of life.

Property for our purposes includes land, goods, money, patents and intellectual creations such as music, art, and literature. The question is how such "things" help us use agency to progress. How can they be motivators?

Consider first the word *gain*. People often confuse it with greed and several scriptures seem to place the word in a negative light …

> "Property provides a sphere of personal sovereignty…. There is an indissoluble connection between private property and individual freedom."
>
> – George Will

Churches … built up to get gain … power … become popular.[9]

Priestcrafts … that they may get gain and praise of the world.[10]

To get gain, to be praised of men.[11]

[T]hey began to seek to get gain that they might be lifted up one above another ….[12]

… but note that it isn't gain itself that is negative, but rather the **improper application** of gain for purposes of praise, popularity, power.

Gain, standing by itself, rightly suggests advancement, growth, improvement. We are motivated to seek gain to improve our lot in life.

In fact, I submit that the acquisition of property of all types is *central* to agency, not peripheral. Property and freedom produce true independence – the essence of agency.

Here's why. The more resources we have …

> … the greater our *freedom*. We have more time to work on other things.

> … the more people are available to *help*. Because of advances inspired from a loving Father, the nation is fed by 2% of us whereas in 1800, 83% of the American labor force was in agriculture.

> … the greater the ability to tinker, experiment, create, and *innovate*. We can spend money on research, consultants, and on supposedly wild ideas to produce improvements for the good of all.

> … the more *latitude* we have. We have the luxury of making mistakes as we experiment and try new things. We have the funds to correct them, not live with them forever after.

> … the greater the *capital formation*. More people have extra money to invest in the products of the future.

About 29 B.C., Nephites and Lamanites opened their lands to one another and they could go wherever they desired "...and thus they did have free intercourse one with another, to buy and to sell, and to **get gain**, according to their desire."[13]

Add Lehi's reassurance to his son Jacob: "... thou knowest the greatness of God; and he shall consecrate thine afflictions **for thy gain**."[14]

Gain is not greed in and of itself, but rather a necessary motivator to prosperity.

Money as Agency Stimulator

For most of history, barter governed the exchange of goods, grains and cattle being the most popular trading items. To progress by tinkering with new innovations, one had to set aside enough edibles to make up for time away from orchard and farm. Possible but difficult.

Then came money, initially in such forms as cowry shells and beads, grains and cattle, pieces of brass, and coins of silver and gold. After travels to China, Marco Polo introduced the idea of paper money to Europeans, but it wasn't until the 1660s during the final years of the Reformation that banknotes were introduced by the Bank of England.[15] Because the Reformation, dating from Luther's 95 theses in 1517 to the late 1600s, was inspired of the Lord as a bridge to the Restoration, could not a more easily handled medium of exchange also have been planned upstairs? If so, one can be quite sure the plan was for intrinsic value rather than nominal value (fiat) currency.

Perhaps the Nephites' use of *both* grain and metals as currency, as explained in Alma 11 – just as the Mesopotamian civilization did in 3000 B.C. – may someday serve again as a model.

Whether bills or coins or digits, money serves two purposes: (1) as a medium of exchange between a seller and a buyer, and (2) as a store of value. The first function muddles along in most countries; the second has a horrible track record everywhere.

This chapter cannot adequately treat even a sliver of information about money that is discussed in economics textbooks. But as it relates to agency, I submit two points about its stimulation power:

Money is private property that, if properly protected, provides its owner with a <u>sufficient sense of security that he is willing to take risks and act</u>. If it holds its value, ideas take life, innovation flourishes, and prosperity spreads.

On the other hand, money is a commodity that governments and central banks <u>can manipulate to the detriment of individual owners</u>. Because the value of the fruits of one's efforts can thereby fade over time, innovation suffers if sufficient stable capital is not assembled to launch new products.

The important point is that easier methods of exchange, trade, and investment facilitate robust agency. If someone today uses his agency to create a good idea, and if currency is stable, there is a great chance it will attract investors. Individuals and societies alike will progress.

Law as Agency Protector

Why should you exercise agency to act if you do not own the resulting product? Why act if you're not sure you will gain and <u>keep</u> the fruits of your labor – that your property will be protected by law?

This especially applies to intellectual property which is much easier to steal than tangible property. Stealing is always wrong, of course, but stealing tangible property stops the moment the property is consumed. Stealing intellectual property with its inherent ability to multiply itself means not only theft of the germane idea, but theft of the fruits that could have followed.

Government's responsibility is to protect the fruits of the labors of those who take risks to be productive. That means a level playing field, protection of patents to reward the inventor and keep poachers at bay, allowing time for the use of a patent without turning it into an unfair monopoly, and preventing government favoritism – cronyism.

If government is weak, we become unsure of receiving the fruits of our labor, ideas, innovations. If government is domineering, we feel less free to experiment and innovate for fear of violating some obscure rule.

Countries that prosper have three traits in common: limited government, economic freedom, and worship of a higher power with its accompanying belief there is good and evil, right and wrong.

When we are confident government exercises the right balance – that efforts will be protected without being a nanny about it – we will think deeply, take risks, and act.

&

And the Lord called his people Zion, because they were of one heart and one mind, and dwelt in righteousness; and there was **no poor among them**.[16]

And Not Be Acted Upon

Chapter 13

Objects
Who Pulls the Strings

"Being acted upon means
somebody else is pulling the strings."
— James E. Faust

"Lucifer's purpose is to make us objects not agents!"
— David A. Bednar

To be acted upon means
others pull your strings.

They make decisions for you
and tell you what to do.

Which discourages creative thinking.

Which saps your initiative
and limits your choices.

Thus intimidating you from acting.

A person who cannot or
will not act is an object.

String pullers – what variety. Some wear religious finery to springboard into political control and become the <u>power behind the throne</u> – Cardinal Richilieu and King Louis XIII of France in the 1600s. Others use lesser offices to achieve the same goal – Chancellor and diplomatic chess champion Otto von Bismarck steering the figurehead German Emperor Wilhelm I, at least until Kaiser Wilhelm II succeeded him and canned the Prussian.[1]

But one historical string-pulling manipulator most closely fits the common image of Satan himself. This evil genius held his country "firmly in the grip of superstition and terror; the arch string-puller behind the scenes. … About this whole person there was something repellent, and this was not due solely to the general uncleanliness of his body and attire, but rather as if he <u>exuded an aura of something evil and sordid</u>, … an aura of great power surrounded him."[2]

This power behind the throne so dominated his nation's titular ruler and ministers that a member of parliament actually employed the puppet visual – that they "have been turned into marionettes, marionettes whose threads have been taken firmly in hand by … the evil genius."[3]

The puppet: Tsar Nicholas II of Russia. The puppeteer: Rasputin.

❧

"He's smart." "She's beautiful." "He's strong."

It's the story of life. We watch. We compare. We compete.

Competing with others is part of progress. Winning brings satisfaction; losing brings sadness. But with defeat can come a determination to try again and do better.

The problem is when competition becomes too intense and negative emotions arise like a summer thunderstorm – envy, jealousy, anger.

Thus it was with Cain and Abel. Cain exhibited all three when his offering was rejected and Abel's accepted. He sought control over Abel and his blessings and wealth. He wanted to reduce Abel to an object. A lifeless object.

Agents, Subjects, Objects

It began with pride and a desire to feel important and bask in adulation – the kicks that come from control of others. The path to the top for some has been intellect and the command of language. **Every villain of the Book of Mormon, for example, was fluent with words and very persuasive.** For others it was beauty, such as Cleopatra. But for most who became the original kings and emperors in their societies, it was muscular strength and success on the battlefield that put them on a throne. The strongest became the kings; wimps need not apply.

> The critical question of a potential leader is how he views his fellow man. Is man an agent unto himself – with the right to decide and the responsibility for the consequences – or an object to be manipulated?

As kings enjoyed royal status, their families maneuvered to extend and sustain. Titles were invented and princes, pointing to their special daddy-provided, training-wheels upbringing, convinced the peasants that kingship qualities were inherited, the famous DNA claim to power.

For centuries, monarchies were the rule – kings reigned and powerful aristocracies executed royal whims. And what should these uppities call those not so privileged? Simple: subjects. The word captures it: subservient, lesser, one under the control of his betters.

So it was until the last half of the 18th century when an upstart gaggle of colonies decided they didn't want to be subjects any more. The U.S. Constitution reversed this and the people for the first time were declared sovereign over their government. Think of that – the first time since Enoch that people as a whole were declared agents unto themselves.

Will it stick?

Some maintain we are in danger of reverting to monarchical ways. Congress and the president may be elected, but increasingly an aristocracy of unelected lawmakers and administrators wields the real day-to-day power and **views people as subjects who can't really govern themselves.**

With over 100,000 federal rules and regulations as their instruments (and an estimated 400,000 if we want to include state and local governments), officious busybodies, faceless and unaccountable, try

to control how Americans behave – they run the show. Especially with social problems such as addictions and family breakups, **they intervene to alleviate bad consequences** under the guise of "we're only trying to help." They deprive people of the opportunity to learn the lessons of mistakes and thus hamper agency and the growth of self-responsible individuals.

The apostle Peter forcefully made the point with an unexpected grouping: "But let none of you suffer as a murderer, or as a thief, or as an evil-doer, or as a busybody in other men's matters."[4]

Such meddlers treat people as subjects rather than independent agents, and if we don't arrest the trend, we will become objects.

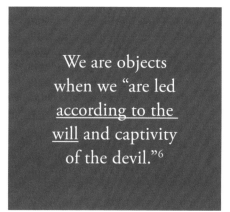

> We are objects when we "are led according to the will and captivity of the devil."[6]

It's not new. Less than five years before Christ's appearance to the Nephites, "there were many merchants in the land, and also many lawyers, and many officers,"[5] officers no doubt meaning government officials. This set the stage for a repeat of the Nephite disease – pride.

What's behind it all?

The famous 121st section of the Doctrine and Covenants bluntly states the matter:

> It is the nature and disposition of almost all men, as soon as they get **a little authority, as they suppose**, they will immediately begin to exercise **unrighteous dominion**.

A universal trait of mankind – get some power and use it over others for your own benefit. The me-first natural man pokes his head above the rest.

So how does a society morph from agents to subjects to objects?

Let's look at four forms of governance:

Class A: Let people **guide** *themselves.* It is the most agency-loyal. People are guided by foundational laws, such as the Ten Commandments, but more importantly follow righteous principles and **become self governing**. As Joseph Smith explained, "I teach them correct principles and they govern themselves."

This is the government of the celestial kingdom. Inhabitants will not be saddled with numerous rules and regulations; they will be advanced enough and guided by love to know how they must act and will not need enforcers to control them. They will be their own enforcers.

Class B: Tell people what they **cannot** *do.* This is probably the best we can achieve on earth. The laws and regulations seek to establish a well-ordered society and **protect life, liberty, and the fruits of one's labor**. The menu ranges from traffic lights to water purity to patent protection to penalties for fisticuffs, but generally conform to common sense and respect for freedoms. The people as sovereign and government as servant remain sacrosanct.

Class C: Tell people what they **can** *do.* People slip into this class when they reason that if government can tell us what we *cannot* do, why should it not have the power to tell us what we *can* do? This faulty logic underlies the spurt to centralized power. The relationship between people as sovereign and government as servant is turned on its head and we are on the road to becoming objects instead of agents. **When government is seen as the source of rights, the slippery slope to tyranny just got another slather of grease**.

*Class D: Tell people what they **must do**.* All societies must establish a few "must do" rules such as military conscription and taxation for infrastructure, but it can become habit forming and in time **the defining feature of tyranny**. When a government can mandate that Catholic nuns pay for contraception coverage in their health-care plan,[7] what stops it from imposing any rule it dreams up?

All of this leads to more rule writing because there will always be imaginative people thirsty to write rules to govern every possible behavior. And exercise power over others.

When a society slips down the rungs from Class A to Class D governance, puppet strings become cables.

Insights to Ponder

Insightful quotes on this matter from four leaders of the Church set the stage for the next chapters of what it means to be acted upon.

Elder D. Todd Christofferson:

"And let us remember, Satan was not volunteering to be our savior. He was not interested in suffering or dying for anyone. He wasn't going to shed any of his blood. **He wanted the glory, honor, and power of God without paying any price.** What he failed to understand or to believe is that one cannot possess the power of God without being the embodiment of justice. Lucifer was seeking for power without goodness. He supposed that he could be a law unto himself, meaning that the law would be whatever he said it was at any given moment and that he could change his mind at any time. In that way, no one could count on anything and **no one would have the ability to be an independent actor**. He would be supreme, and no one else could advance."[8]

Elder Neal A. Maxwell:

"The more we sin, the more we are acted upon, eventually **coming to be almost like inanimate objects** that are acted upon. ... [O]nly the righteous are fully free. Each wrong choice, which we freely make, makes us less free and more acted upon."[9]

Elder David A. Bednar:

"Learning by faith and from experience are two of the central features of the Father's plan of happiness. The Savior preserved moral agency through the Atonement and made it possible for us to act and to learn by faith. Lucifer's rebellion against the plan sought to destroy the agency of man, and **his intent was that we as learners would only be acted upon**."[10]

At the beginning of this chapter, I quoted President James E. Faust saying, "Being acted upon means somebody else is pulling the strings." He went on to say that in his years of practicing law…

"… some individuals **did not think they were responsible** or guilty in any way even though they had violated a law. They felt they were not to be blamed [that] it was really their parents' fault because they were not properly taught, or it was society's fault because they were never given a chance in life. So often they had some reason or excuse for blaming their actions on someone or something else rather than accepting the responsibility for their own actions. **They did not act for themselves but were acted upon.** … Our moral agency requires us to know good from evil and choose the good. If we are trying to avoid not only evil but the very appearance of evil, we will act for ourselves and not be acted upon."[11]

Satan's Stepladder

Satan wants either a highly ordered state where everyone must follow his dictates or, failing that, a disorderly state where confusion reigns and people do not progress. Anarchy or totalitarianism with smothering regulations, he works with either extreme. The last thing he wants is reasonable balance between the two.

He gradually brings us into submission through six stages:

Intellectualism – puff up and put down.
Pride and the worship of the three-pound god between the ears produces self-certified elites. Their status lures followers.

  ✔ You still decide your own actions.

Distortion – change meaning.
Pressure to conform with politically correct thinking distorts meaning, homogenizes natural differences, and splinters natural unity.

  ✔ Judicial force to conform begins to appear.

Centralization – concentrate power and subvert.
A moderate amount furthers an orderly society, but excess concentration leads to abuse.

  ✔ Agency copes but deterioration lurks.

Statism – sap individual will.
Governments by nature expand and numerous rules tell people what they must do. They overreach and usurp.

  ✔ Agency teeters.

Socialism – destroy agency.

Numerous variations try to disguise the common goal of equality through coercion. If Satan were to vote in our elections, I doubt he would vote for a free-market advocate.

- ✔ Man's agency is socialism's enemy.

Tyranny – dictate and control.

Through surveillance, fear, and shrewd demonstrations of violent power, dictators control every aspect of society.

- ✔ Except for the power to think, man's agency ceases to exist and he becomes an object.

To determine society's present stage, ask yourself, "How free am I to run my own life? How many things am I left alone to decide? How much are others telling me what I can and cannot do, and especially what I must do?"

As you do, remember that Satan did not woo a third of the hosts of heaven by playing the heavy. Rather, **he promised a no-effort paradise**.

> When we allow ourselves to feel offended, we allow ourselves to be acted upon.

He took advantage of those afraid to be their own agents and take risks. He flattered them saying they were already good enough and need not trudge through a messy mortality. He enticed those who wanted a guaranteed return ticket and used the ploy to grab power and attempt to overthrow the Father.

His goals and strategy have not changed. Turn agents into objects. The step-by-step process we examine in the following chapters works on all too many people.

Distinguish Between People and Behavior

Against the elaborate devices Satan has set in motion, we must act forcefully to prevent becoming objects he can manipulate. So what are the guidelines God would have us follow?

Consider two simple questions:

Does God hate Satan? No. He loves all His children.

Does God hate Satan's behavior? Yes. He hates sin in all its forms.

> "For this purpose the Son of God was manifested, that he might destroy the works of the devil."[12]

That obviously must be our guideline as well – love others deeply while opposing sinful behavior. Simple to say, but it takes work.

To weaken our strategy, the world conflates the two: "If you hate what I do, it means you hate me." In other words, the sin and the sinner are the same.

Given such faulty logic, how do we with love defend agency and prevent being acted upon? Three points:

- We must know the opposition, their strategies, their tactics.
- We must be assertive. Effective defense cannot be passive.
- We must apply a variety of educational and persuasional techniques.

On that last point, God Himself persuades, chides, and even derides:

"No power or influence can or ought to be maintained by virtue of the priesthood only by persuasion, by long-suffering, by gentleness and meekness, and by love unfeigned..."[13]

"If thy brother trespass against thee, rebuke him; and if he repent, forgive him."[14]

"[T]he Lord shall have them in derision."[15]

So with us. We must identify wrongs and boldly challenge worldly wisdom. In so doing, we debate without being mean. We stand for right without being belligerent. We fight sinful behavior without hating the behaver. And we can use humor and ridicule just as the Savior did with the parable of gnats and camels.

> Why not have ridicule join forces with reason?

The following six chapters represent battlefields on which we are called to action. (Hymns such as *We Are All Enlisted*; *Onward, Christian Soldiers*; and *Behold a Royal Army* weren't composed for no reason.) The goal during the conflict, of course, is to love even when we must oppose.

To repeat: Distinguish between the person and improper behavior – love the one, hate the other.

And if you find it difficult to love your enemies, at least feel sorry for them.

❧

"If we did not have moral agency, we would simply be puppets manipulated by strings of fate."
– David A. Bednar

Chapter 14

Intellectualism
Worship of the Mind

"For the wisdom of this world is foolishness with God."
— Paul

"Don't use any big words for a few weeks."

When the intellectually gifted set aside the spiritual mechanism
for uncovering truths and the ensuing counsels of God
they could enjoy, their wisdom becomes foolishness.
They become puffed up with what their <u>five</u> senses tell them,
and mock as hicks those who use <u>six</u> senses to gain knowledge.

Some people thank God for their
accomplishments and worship Him.

Others thank themselves and worship
the three-pound god between their ears.

Intellectualism thus begins with pride
— my three-pound god is smarter
than your three-pound god.

Intellectuals who worship their own minds
come to believe everything is relative
and there are no absolute truths.

With no absolute truths and the mind of man
as the highest power, the stage is set for the
self-anointed to tell others what to do.

It's called intellectualism.

A journal article out of the University of Oregon described a government-funded study that, well, … you figure it out:

> Merging feminist postcolonial science studies and feminist political ecology, the feminist glaciology framework generates robust analysis of gender, power, and epistemologies in dynamic social-ecological systems, thereby leading to more just and equitable science and human-ice interactions.[1]

Feminist glaciology framework? Human-ice interactions? So, was the Titanic sunk by a male iceberg or a female iceberg?

❧

I define "intellectualism" as the improper application of intellect – the worship of the mind – and therefore see myself as part of the anti-intellectualism movement.

Contributors to a Wikipedia article on this topic, on the other hand, define anti-intellectualism as "hostility to and mistrust of intellect, intellectuals, and intellectualism commonly expressed as deprecation of education and philosophy, and the dismissal of art, literature, and science as impractical and even contemptible human pursuits."[2]

So when we say we oppose worship-of-the-mind intellectualism, these people distort "anti-intellectualism" as "anti-intellectual." They lump intellect, intellectuals and intellectualism together thus combining a quality, a person, and a use as if they were one thing. Their cunning manipulation suggests those who oppose intellectualism are really opposing intellect and knowledge, and are therefore ignorant rubes.

Three definitions help clarify:

1. Intelligence is a <u>quality</u>. We should work diligently and become as intelligent and knowledgeable as possible.

2. Intellectual can be a <u>trait</u> or a <u>person</u>. We give proper due to those of intellectual prowess in equal measure as we respect the accomplishments of the tradesman, the laborer, or anyone else.

3. Intellectualism is an <u>application</u>. It is the use of intellectual ability for purposes God would not approve such as worship of the mind with its corresponding decrease in worship of Him.

To emphasize, **intellectualism is not the quality of being intelligent.** It is, rather, the **improper use of intellectual ability** to achieve fame and power. It is the prideful assumption that such attainment is reason to rule over others – the puffed-up "I am smarter than you and deserve lofty status" ploy.

We have been commanded from the beginning to acquire knowledge, think carefully, and then act, and through those actions produce the best inventions; the best music, literature, and art; the environments for learning; and the best goods and services in a free-market society.

"Historically, and in our own day, some people reject the gospel of Jesus Christ because, in their view, it doesn't have adequate intellectual sophistication."

– Quentin L. Cook

Somewhere along the road, however, cars sputtered. Jacob elaborates:

O the <u>vainness, and the frailties, and the foolishness</u> of men! When they are learned they think they are wise, and they hearken not unto the counsel of God, for they set it aside, supposing they know of themselves, wherefore, their wisdom is foolishness and it profiteth them not.[3]

That multiple scriptures warn about worldly wisdom indicates its malignancy:

- Let not the wise man glory in his wisdom.[4]

- Professing themselves to be wise, they became fools ....[5]

- For the wisdom of this world is foolishness with God.[6]

- Beware lest any man spoil you through philosophy and vain deceit.[7]

- For men shall be lovers of their own selves ... **Ever learning, and never able to come to the knowledge of the truth**.[8]

God wants us to progress – "to be learned is good if they hearken unto the counsels of God"[9] – so the danger is not in the **gaining** of knowledge, but in the false pride of **worshiping** oneself for holding an academic degree or other intellectual achievement and refusing to use all God-given paths to knowledge.

Let's look at three applications:

1. Occupational Elitism and Aristocracies

2. Academic Elitism with Pomp and Silliness

3. Religious Elitism including Priestcraft and Secularism

Occupation Elitism

And the people began to be distinguished by ranks, according to their riches and their chances for learning; yea, some were ignorant because of their poverty, and others did receive great learning because of their riches.[10]

My father-in-law, a county attorney and rancher, told what happened when an expert from the Department of Agriculture in Washington visited southern Idaho to tell farmers and ranchers how to improve their lot in life. Commenting on lamb production, this expert told the poor benighted folks, "Your problem is that all the lambs are born in the spring. You have to get the ewes [he pronounced it "EE-weez"] to produce lambs uniformly throughout the year."

He was hooted out of the room.

Why did this man think that his college degree and his title in a government agency gave him superior knowledge to people laboring daily in the field? If there's a major symptom of pride, it's the arrogant belief that people can't run their own lives and must be told by a class of enlightened ones what to think and what to do.

Similarly, I once asked a journalism major why he chose to pursue that career. He answered, "Because I want to change the world." Stupid me. I thought the role of journalists was to report the facts, not to drive change by spinning the news. The belief, again, that people aren't smart enough to analyze events properly.

King Mosiah noted the normal good-evil distribution and gave this guiding principle:

> Now it is not common that the voice of the people desireth anything contrary to that which is right; but it is common for the lesser part of the people to desire that which is not right; therefore this shall ye observe and make it your law – to do your business by the voice of the people.[11]

But the king-men of Zarahemla rejected this counsel and felt entitled to govern because of who their parents were:

> Now those who were in favor of kings were **those of high birth**, and they sought to be kings; and they were **supported by those who sought power and authority** over the people.[12]

Class elitism and hereditary privilege have plagued societies for centuries. When ambitious immigrants boarded rickety ships to sail the treacherous North Atlantic to America, they came to escape the smothering royalty and aristocracies of their countries of birth and the dearth of opportunity. They wanted to work, enjoy the fruits of their labors, and to be judged by their accomplishments, not by their DNA. They and we, their descendants, prospered. Yet we now have intellectuals establishing **a new aristocracy for fame, deference, power, and gain.** The very reason our ancestors fled.

Many who stayed behind share blame for the continuation of monarchies because they became comfortable being subjects instead of free-will actors. They even became enthralled with the doings of their higher-ups – "I wonder what the king is doing tonight; what merriment is the king pursuing tonight?"[13]

Intellectualism grows because many Americans yearn for royalty – idols to worship be they in sports, movies, music, politics, or business. Ever notice how many today are fascinated with the "royal families" in the lands their forefathers left? Even those who claim to believe in a universal King are still drawn into the adulation of the rich and famous.

Academic Elitism

One professor to another: "It works in reality, I wonder if it works in theory."

How a person views who or what is the highest power in the universe sets the framework. A December 2017 survey of some 4700 Americans by Pew Research Center found that …[14]

56% believe in God as described in the Bible

33% believe in some other higher power / spiritual force

10% do not believe in any higher power / spiritual force

Here's the breakout by groups:

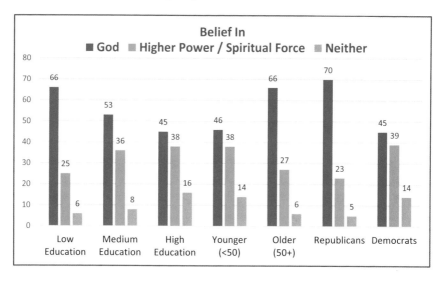

While a plurality of the higher educated believes in God, 16% are outright atheists and a substantial 38% believe in a less-well-defined higher power or spiritual force. Contenders for the latter could be a wispy and formless being, the arc of history, The Force from *Star Wars*, the Eternal Flame from *Thor: Ragnarok*, or … the human mind.

> "Students are unlikely to go through college without being assigned to read *The Communist Manifesto* … while a classic like *The Federalist* is seldom assigned reading …."
>
> – Thomas Sowell

If God is the highest power, then all else must be submissive to His requirements (the Ten Commandments at a minimum) and the selfish ambitions of men are somewhat constrained. But if the mind of man is deemed the highest power, then it's "Katy bar the door" as mental megahertz, cunning, and the management of the creature determine the winners.

With such a belief, one's behavior need only be guided by one's desires, subservient to no one.

Most college professors in the social sciences fit the previously illustrated demographics that show a distinct leaning toward non-God explanations of the universe. By one study, Democratic professors outnumber Republican professors by an 8:1 margin.[15] Another study found that 62% of philosophy professors are atheists.[16] And in a 2007 study of professors, a majority claim belief in God, but are three times more likely to claim atheism than the average American. The percentage of atheists among the total population has increased in the last decade and we can assume it has also increased among the professoriate, very probably with no change in the 3:1 ratio.[17]

> "The one who learns and learns and doesn't practice is like the one who plows and plows and never plants."
>
> – Plato

Almost every one of my colleagues in graduate school had been students continually, save summers, since kindergarten. The moment they graduated, they reversed the roles and began teaching. Teaching what they had been taught. Very little if any real world experience.

Insular, repetitive, passing along the settled philosophies of the erudite with fewer and fewer voices that challenge and present other points of view are the traits of today's universities. Former Stanford University Provost John Etchemendy described the problem to the university's board of trustees in 2017:

> "Over the years, I have watched a growing intolerance at universities ... a kind of intellectual intolerance, a political one-sidedness, that is the antithesis of what universities should stand for. ... **Universities must remain open**

forums for contentious debate, and they cannot do so while officially espousing one side of that debate. … We need to encourage real diversity of thought in the professoriate and that will be even harder to achieve. It is hard for anyone to acknowledge high-quality work when that work is at odds, perhaps opposed, to one's own deeply held beliefs. But we all need worthy opponents to challenge us in our search for truth. It is absolutely essential to the quality of our enterprise."[18]

At least one university official gets it.

Don't get me wrong. My congratulations to those who have advanced degrees; they worked hard. But I take issue with those who smugly assume such attainment places them higher up some revered pecking order and makes them better than, say, those who work with their hands.

A plumber once handled a problem at my home. As he wrote the date and the word "installed" on a new water heater, he made the "d" with an upstroke but did not complete the downstroke, a feature handwriting analysts call the "genius d." I finally teased out of him that he had indeed scored in the genius range on a high school intelligence test. But, he said, one quarter of college was all he could stand; he had to be working with his hands to find satisfaction.

Pomp and Silliness

Many God-fearing, next-door-neighbor types in academia and related professions discover, create, invent, and add to our body of knowledge, all without being puffed up about it. A tip of the hat to them. The physical and medical sciences are especially good; economic and business studies are usually productive; but the social sciences are often silly and pea-soupy.

Ground-breaking discoveries are difficult to come by, but contributing new words to the intelligentsia vocabulary is easy. Such rung-climbers need not be thoroughly grounded in what they prattle about; they merely must **wade in complex matters to convey an image of a complex, deep thinker.**

Even a casual skimming of proposed research and dissertations in the social sciences uncovers hilarious gobbledygook:

> "There are some ideas so absurd that only an intellectual could believe them."
>
> – George Orwell

Feminist-posthumanist intersectionality

Balances discursive and material elements

Teleological historiography

Duoethnography and constructed gendered subjectivities

Cultivate an interiority

Ambivalently embodied neoliberal logic

Counterhegemonic status

Practices of normalization, solipsism, and ontological expansiveness

Salsa genders that defer heteronormativity

And get a load of this sentence:

"In the course of reanimating thermodynamic motifs in Marx's labor power metabolics and Freud's trauma energetics, the essay broaches entropics as a poetics of depletion that offsets affect theories promoting open-system metaphors."[19]

As one wag put it, "Intellectuals use fancy words so they'll sound perspicacious."

Sometimes the individual words are understandable, but the application is, to be generous, less than useful:

> Such socio-spatial practices are the means through which men, women, chickens and cattle become privileged and/or othered within dominant gender-species hierarchical arrangements.[21]

So, do privileged chickens taste better than regular ones?

In today's social-science academia, **unintelligible gobbledygook is looked upon as profound, chin-stroking brilliance.** It's reminiscent of people who **"despised the words of plainness and sought for things they could not understand."**[22] Also:

> **... and how blind and impenetrable are the understandings of the children of men; for they will not seek wisdom ....**[23]

As one academic said about a colleague: "On the surface he's profound, but deep down, he's superficial."[20]

I wonder whether the subconscious reasoning of the would-be intellectual runs like this: "If the works of God are incomprehensible to man, I'll make my works incomprehensible so I'll be viewed as god-like."

As for pomp, color, and costume, baccalaureate ceremonies at universities come close to gatherings of monarchies in old countries. Looks like a bomb went off in a paint shop.

Impenetrable, dense, incomprehensible, convoluted writings, intellectual stupidity. Complexity is profundity. All in the category of the vain imaginations constituting the great and spacious building – the pride and wisdom of the world.[24]

Religious Elitism

> [P]riestcrafts are that men preach and set themselves up for a light unto the world, that they may get gain and praise of the world ....[25]

As people in Nephite times began to be distinguished by ranks, "Satan had great power, unto the stirring up of the people to do all manner of iniquity, and to the puffing them up with pride, tempting them to seek for **power, and authority, and riches, and the vain things** of the world."[26]

Nehor is the go-to example for all of this[27] – a major villain in the Book of Mormon who started a church instead of raising an army. He…

- Preached what he pretended to be the word of God;

- Taught that all mankind will be saved and have eternal life;

- Declared priests and teachers ought to become popular, and should not labor with their hands but be supported by the people;

- Became popular and prideful;

- Persuaded people to support him and give him money;

- Began to wear very costly apparel;

- Established a church after the manner of his preaching; and

- Endeavored to enforce priestcraft by the sword.

Those who followed Nehor's formula "loved the vain things of the world, and they went forth preaching false doctrines ... for the sake of riches and honor." They still do today.

We also know that priestcraft churches "shall teach with their learning ... vain and foolish doctrines, and shall be puffed up in their hearts ...."[28]

Costly apparel, among other vain things of the world, has always been associated with elites – those in the Savior's words who are gorgeously appareled and live delicately in kings' courts[29] – including priestcraft churches that foster class distinctions and put down so-called lessers, such as with the Zoramites in Alma 32.

Moroni saw the day when his record would come forth and was unsparing in his speech to the priestcraft practitioners that will be among us.

> Yea, it shall come in a day when the power of God shall be denied, and churches become defiled and ... leaders of churches and teachers shall rise in the **pride** of their hearts ....
>
> ... when there shall be churches built up that shall say: Come unto me, and for your money you shall be forgiven of your sins.
>
> ... why have ye built up churches unto yourselves to get **gain**? Why have ye transfigured the holy word of God ...?
>
> ... ye walk in the pride of your hearts ... unto the wearing of very **fine apparel**, unto envying, and strifes, and malice, and persecutions, and all manner of **iniquities**; and your churches, yea, even every one, have become **polluted** because of the pride of your hearts.
>
> ... ye do love money, and your substance, and your fine apparel, and the **adorning** of your churches, more than ye love the poor ....[30]

The examples abound: A New Orleans televangelist wants his followers to pay for a $54,000,000 private jet, his fourth.[31] One minister owns 13 mansions and a $100,000 mobile home for her dogs. Multi-million dollar mansions and million-dollar annual salaries are not unusual among mega-church pastors.[32]

Consider the man who starts his own church. He becomes a leader, the one in authority. He uses scripture to exercise power. As a small businessman, he relies on cash-in-the-plate donations but seeks mega-church status and the riches that can bring. Rich or poor, he achieves status. To be dressed in finery symbolic of authority and paid to put one's own spin on scriptures is heady stuff.

Secular Religion

As cultural elites disparage religion as superstition, and as fewer Americans associate with an organized religion, the trend toward secularism accelerates – absolute and not open to debate.

This secularization especially appeals to those who seek organizations that will worship their IQs and initials following their names. (I once saw an article where the author listed "Ph.D., N.C.C., D.C.M.H.S., L.M.H.C." after her name.) They play leading roles in federal, state, and local bureaucracies and are contributing significantly to the rise of the administrative state. They have become the intellectual priesthood of a secular religion.

Compare those who worship God to those who worship the mind.

A believer's foundation is an unmovable Deity. A truth will be a truth yesterday, today, and tomorrow. There are absolutes. Right will always be right; wrong will always be wrong. The believer gets these truths from what God has said in the scriptures and from prophets. Knowing he will someday stand accountable before God, the believer develops standards, morals, and behaviors consistent with those beliefs.

> "Have the courage to have your wisdom regarded as stupidity. ... And have the courage to suffer the contempt of the sophisticated world."
>
> – Antonin Scalia

A <u>mind worshiper's foundation</u>, in comparison, is less stable because it is conditioned on circumstances – ever-changing circumstances. It is the slippery concept of moral relativity – no absolutes, no unchanging truths, no right and wrong, no good and evil. All things are relative and they become their own highest authority. The result is a rickety structure that tilts this way and that depending on fads, winds of doctrine, trendy cotton-candy theories, peer pressures, and political correctness. Charles Dickens observed: "Moral relativism has set in so deeply that the gilded classes have become incapable of discerning right from wrong. … Life is one **great moral mush** ...."[33]

> But the natural man receiveth not the things of the Spirit of God: for they are foolishness unto him: neither can he know them, because they are spiritually discerned.[34]

The relativism in secular religion has made it easier to discount consequences, justice, mercy, and even the Atonement itself, and offers a convenient hide-behind for those wanting to escape responsibility for their actions. If someone buys that good and evil are imaginary constructs – that nothing can be absolutely true but only relatively valid or invalid depending upon a frame of reference and circumstances – then that someone will fail a major test of mortality.

President Dallin H. Oaks in 2014:

> "The rejection of an unprovable God and the denial of right and wrong is most influential in the world of higher education. Secular humanism … is deliberately or inadvertently embodied in the teachings of faculty members in many colleges and universities. … [T]he objectionable element in the various humanist manifestos is their rejection of the existence of God and their denial of the moral absolutes rooted

in His commandments. … **[M]any of today's Christian *ministers* cannot truthfully affirm their belief in God.**"[35]

Followers of Jesus Christ become self-governing. They accept and follow principles, not pharisaical rules.

The absence of eternal principles, on the other hand, leads to ever stronger efforts for society to control its citizens. Secularists try to cure societal ills by issuing more and more rules, which in turn destroys the idea of responsibility and accountability, and fosters rationalization. **People become "other governed" and believe that everything is okay as long as they don't violate a written rule.** (More on this in Chapter 17.)

President Oaks observes in today's world: "There is no accountability beyond what man's laws or public disapproval impose on those who are caught."[36]

Similarly, Archbishop of Chicago Francis Cardinal George warns that "this tendency for the government to claim for itself authority over all areas of human experience forms the secularization of our culture. If God cannot be part of public life, then the state itself plays God."[37] G.K. Chesterton adds, "Dethrone God and the state becomes God."[38]

The tragedy of the intellectualism of secular religion is it becomes a stepping stone to statism and socialism and leads to smothering government.

❦

For the wisdom of their wise men shall perish, and
the understanding of their prudent men shall be hid.[39]

Chapter 15

Distortion
Corrupting the Culture

"Lucifer's only hope of success [is] to achieve a paradigm shift or values inversion – in other words, to characterize the Father's plan as resulting in grief and misery and Lucifer's plan as resulting in joy and happiness."
– Quentin L. Cook

The adversary's goal is to condition, sensitize, and inoculate people against the true meaning of words, thus misleading them.

Gender, marriage, and family are
gifts from God, have been defined by Him,
and are essential to our eternal progress.

Satan is distorting man's centuries-long
understanding of them.

Whatever is said in defense of these gifts is
no longer treated as legitimate opinion,
but often labeled hate speech.

Aggressively enflamed definitions of hate speech
thus spawn demand for restrictions.

As the definition of hate speech expands,
the religious become targets and
religious freedom is undermined.

Gender, marriage, and family issues are
the critical arenas in today's war with evil.

I n May 2019, track star CeCe Telfer from Franklin Pierce University in New Hampshire won an NCAA women's track national championship in the 400 meter hurdles contest beating out eight other contenders.

A year earlier, Telfer was competing in track meets as … a man.

NCAA rules allow male athletes to compete as women if they suppress their testosterone levels for a full calendar year.[1]

❧

Such head-shaking departures from traditional events and under-standings begin with changes in the instruments that convey meaning – those little things called words.

Whoever controls the meaning of a word gains the advantage.

Double Meanings Kick It Off

Ever wonder why slim chance and fat chance mean the same thing?

Language constantly changes. We find the funny, the helpful, the idiosyncratic and, depending on usage, the same word or phrase can even have opposite meanings:[2]

We toss out bad food but toss out good ideas.

The men have left and the women are left.

The full moon was out when the lights went out.

This car could really go until it started to go.

Some people multiply words to obfuscate meaning: "You are in an orderly transition between career changes while undergoing a period of non-waged involuntary leisure during your temporary outplacement." In simpler words, "You're fired."

Fancy speak dresses things up:

A recession is negative economic growth.

The homeless are involuntarily undomiciled.

The unemployed are economically marginalized.

An environmental hygienist is a janitor.

And used cars are now pre-owned vehicles.

New words cascade endlessly upon us. In recent years we've become accustomed to bitcoins, emojis, paywalls, staycations, and upcycles.

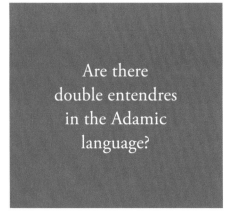

Are there double entendres in the Adamic language?

We have megachurches and microaggressions and memes. People around us may be sheeple, muggles, or noobs who get "pwned" (soundly defeated). We ping, tweet, hashtag, unfriend; we take selfies and usies. We're woke. Meh.

Word changes and newcomers are the pattern of history and most are harmless. But beyond the natural evolution of language where slang becomes mainstream, we are warned about those …

… that call evil good, and good evil; that put darkness for light, and light for darkness; that put bitter for sweet, and sweet for bitter![3]

And …

Wherefore, take heed … that ye do not judge that which is evil to be of God, or that which is good and of God to be of the devil.[4]

That Isaiah and Moroni would so warn indicates we face insidious inroads into our ways of thinking and speaking that corrupt culture and weaken agency.

Let's examine the adversary's distortion tools.

Soften the Bad

Clever replacements (more than synonyms; slang-onyms) blur meaning and minimize the severity of sin.

Steal	Swipe, filch, nab, cop, loot, pinch, lift.
Murder	Hit, wipe, snuff, eliminate, clip, frag, rip, zap, erase.
Adultery	Cheat, step out, affair, philander, play around – swingers, throuples, open relationships.

At times it's even a 180 degree reversal.

Hack	Previously all negative, it was a slash, hit, an attack on your computer, someone not particularly great at what he does. Now it's being used as a positive, such as a tip, a suggestion, a new piece of knowledge.
Bad	In today's slang can mean good or great.
Wicked	Has always been a negative, but now has morphed into a positive intensifier, such as wicked good.
Dope	Traditionally meant stupid but now used as awesome or great.
Sick	Can now also mean really amazing.
Crash	Can also mean to stay with.
Kill	As it pertains to, say, a homework assignment, "I killed it" means "I got it done" or "I really did a good job on it."

When blurring the meaning of words robs concepts of clarity, people may begin to doubt their undergirding institutions, their own sense of self, and even their traditional values.

Erase Stigmas

Some words that carry a stigma are shifted toward the positive through little steps.

For example, an excess money supply can lead to undesirable consequences, and a commodity that government can create for the price of paper makes many uncomfortable.[5] So *printing money* became *monetizing the debt* and is now called *quantitative easing*, an opaque phrase with airs if there ever was one.

> And at the time that Mosiah discovered them, ... their language had become corrupted ...[6]

Similarly, *dole* became *welfare* became *relief* became *assistance* became *entitlement*. Great irony, that. A title has value and, except for aristocratic inheritance, results from effort such as earning a degree. It is one thing to remove a stigma, quite another to make it a lofty honor.

The word *whoredom* has almost disappeared. *Whores* became *prostitutes*, then *streetwalkers*, then *ladies of the night*, and now are *escorts*. Talk about cheapening a noble word. And *perversion* is now simply an *alternative lifestyle*.

The pattern also pertains to symbols. Perhaps people will become so religiously desensitized and so secularly conditioned that they won't recognize divine warnings contained in prophesied weather events, but merely chalk them up to climate change.

Control the Frame

He who controls how a topic is framed will usually win the debate.

One researcher had participants solve certain situations after reading a word chain. Group A saw the word "skyscraper" first followed by "prayer," while Group B had the two words reversed. The third and fourth words in the chains were "temple" and "cathedral," which have both religious and architectural connotations:

> When 'skyscraper' was listed first, subjects tended to come up with architectural concepts, and when 'prayer' was transposed with 'skyscraper' and listed first, it increased the likelihood of a religious direction.[7]

Similarly, if a man asks if he can smoke while he prays, he will be judged differently than if he asks if he can pray while he smokes. Order counts.

In short, the first words used in an article or speech set the frame for what follows. The early word gets the form, so to speak.

Usurp Good Words

Hijack a plane and you're front-page news. Hijack a God-given word and the world shrugs.

> *Love.* The standard is clear: love one another as God and the Savior love us. But the word has been cheapened and kidnapped, and now means whatever one feels an attraction for or gets a kick out of, be it positive or negative: love to drink, love to get high, love to play around, love to swindle someone, love to boss others, and so forth. Love has come to mean anything the world wants it to be.

Equality. As discussed in several chapters in this book, the battle is between those who use the word to affirm equality of *opportunity* and those who desire equality of *outcome* no matter the effort.

Freedom. Freedom is obviously an essential element of agency. But too many now incorrectly view it as a right to do whatever one wishes (and here's the kicker) ... without consequence. Unfortunately, liberty and libertine (philanderer) stem from the same Latin root.

Choice. Integral as can be to the whole concept of agency, but it's been co-opted in the phrase "pro-choice." After all, who can be anti-choice? People have agency and as a couple can choose how their procreative powers are engaged (save for rape and incest). The masquerade involves consequences and abortion as the escape of choice, so to speak. Looking behind the curtain, **pro-choice in today's parlance actually means anti-consequence**. People conveniently forget choice happens the night before, not the morning after.

> "The slogan or sound bite 'pro-choice' has had an almost magical effect in justifying abortion and in neutralizing opposition to it."
>
> – Dallin H. Oaks

Diversity. A range or variety of things, such as the numerous species of trees and plants that beautified the Garden of Eden and thence the earth for the enjoyment of man. Mendelssohn said, "The essence of beauty is unity in variety." But now it's an excuse to <u>diverge</u> from a traditional value, to mix pluses and minuses, but nonetheless demand to be accepted, thus negating unity. As this trend continues, we have ironic reversal – those who diverged from traditional values now oppose on grounds of diversity those who diverge from their divergence.

Inclusive. Traditionally meant comprehensive and inviting – a non-coerced gesture of kindness to gather those who share common values. Some with differing values now use the word to demand not only entry but also approval. We Latter-day Saints are inclusive of other religions, for example, when giving humanitarian service, but not in softening doctrine. Those who try to include different doctrines in an ecumenical statement of belief end up with mush.

> The word "variety" is not found in the Book of Mormon, but the phrase "all manner of" appears 110 times. The "what" includes seeds, tools, food, clothing, ores, wood, grain, fruit, and ... words.

Tolerance. We grant all people the freedom to run their own lives even if we disagree with their choices. We accept them as children of God and tolerate our differences. But tolerance, according to our changing mores, is now more than putting up with differences. As with inclusiveness, it's on its way to mean acceptance and approval of opposite beliefs or practices, else be flogged with the hate word *intolerant*.

Discrimination. Once indicative of an appreciation of finer things – a discriminating taste was seen as positive – it now means hatred toward one category of people or another.

As striking as the above examples may be, perhaps the prime example of dressing sin in attractive clothing, and to condition people to accept what they normally would not, is the behavior associated with the word gay. Homosexual as a term was rejected by those with same-sex attraction because it was too clinical and sounded like a disorder. Gay, on the other hand, had the connotation of joy, happy, carefree, cheerful, bright, and showy and first appeared on the scene in the early 20th century.[8]

The path was predictable. Activist gays first postured themselves as victims of bigotry and asked for tolerance. Then came equality – that we're all entitled to equal treatment by society. Then acceptance – love me who I am; I'm as good as anyone else.

No arguments to this point.

But then the big step: **not just acceptance but approval** and by this they do not mean mere approval as equal citizens, but **approval of the behavior** that sets them apart – distinguishes them, if you please, as a protected class. Failing to approve of the lifestyle and the teaching of it to schoolchildren, in their logic chain, means you're intolerant, bigoted, and hateful.

"Some people's idea of free speech is that they are free to say what they like, but if anyone says anything back, that is an outrage."

– Winston Churchill

Certain words, however, cannot be completely co-opted because of stronger and broader concepts that stand behind them. In such cases, opponents of God's original definitions try to blur and dilute. Four gifts and principles are the battlefields:

Gender

Marriage

Family

Religion

Gender: Homogenize the Differences

The single most important difference among God's children is our clear, distinct, God-given, biological gender. It used to be called sex, but because of that word's dual meaning, society settled on gender, which unfortunately **opened the mischief door**. As one meme has it, "God created two genders; Satan created the rest." To list a few gay activists have suggested ...

Gender variant, non-binary, neutrois, trans, cisgenderheteronormative, pangender, gender fluid, trans female, two-spirit, other, agender, androgynous, intersex person, genderqueer, gender neutral, transmasculine, transmale, male-to-female, neither, gender questioning, gender nonconforming, bigender, and androgyne.

> Korihor's preaching caused people "to lift up their heads in their wickedness...."[9] Might this describe gay pride?

Facebook at one point had 71 gender options from which to choose, but has now settled for male, female, and "custom."

Yea, they did ... afflict them with all manner of words ....[10]

President Dallin H. Oaks nailed the adversary's plan of action:

"Our knowledge of God's revealed plan of salvation requires us to oppose current social and legal pressures to retreat from traditional marriage and to make changes that **confuse or alter gender or homogenize the differences** between men and women. We know that the relationships, identities, and functions of men and women are essential to accomplish God's great plan."[11]

To confuse and alter gender, radicals demand traditional pronouns be eliminated and replaced with gender-neutral "words":[12]

He/She must be replaced by Zie, Sie, Ey, Ve, Tey or E.

Him/Her now becomes Zim, Sie, Em, Ver, Ter or Em.

> If you don't agree that gender is fluid, you are demonized as a bigoted, homophobic chauvinist, among other juicy labels.

But for outright blasphemy, it's hard to top Duke and Vanderbilt divinity schools – divinity schools! – telling their professors to use "gender-neutral language" when referring to God "to mitigate sexism."[13] Vain imaginations of those in the large and spacious building.

The homogenizing of differences grows from the politically correct idea of self-identity through feelings – that how a person feels is more important than what reality (XX and XY biology) says.

To parallel the idea into other situations, it gets ridiculous …

- If I am 14 and want to drive a car, can I self-identify as 16 and hit the gas? Or if I am 55 but feel 65 (which is not unusual, by the way), can I get Social Security?

- If I am brain injured with a low IQ, can I self-identify as a genius and expect Stanford to accept me?

- If I think I'm a good football quarterback, can I self-identify as an NFL star? (Come to think of it, where's my paycheck?)

But somehow if I'm a boy and want to use the girls' restroom, I can self-identify as a girl and walk right in? And play on the girls' high school basketball team? How absurd is it going to get?

The first words you probably heard in this life pronounced your gender: "It's a boy" or "It's a girl." Yet 44% of all Americans in a recent Pew research survey said someone can be a man or a woman *even if that is different from the sex they were assigned at birth*, while a slight majority 54% said it is determined by the sex assigned at birth.[14]

Consider the facts: The average body has 37 **trillion** cells[15] and each one contains 23 chromosome pairs, the last of which is either an XX or XY denoting gender.[16] <u>A person's sex is stamped on every single cell of the body.</u>

So why do 44% of our fellow Americans think feelings are more important than facts? Obviously we must love all mankind just as our Father does, but we must also defend basic truths such as the origin of gender as it is central to achieving our full, divine potential. *The Family: A Proclamation to the World* states unequivocally that we are all beloved sons or daughters – two categories only – of heavenly parents and that gender "is an essential characteristic of individual premortal, mortal, and eternal identity and purpose."[17]

Satan must be relishing in this identity kerfuffle he has fostered of late. Which leads one to wonder whether there's a whiff of Mosiah's warning going on here?

> And if the time comes that the voice of the people doth choose iniquity, then is the time that the judgments of God will come upon you; yea, then is the time he will visit you with great destruction even as he has hitherto visited this land.[18]

Marriage: Share the Definition

While homogenizing differences, Satan attacks unity, principally the one that will last for eternity if correctly performed and honored.

Brigham Young:

"[T]he marriage relation … lays the foundation for worlds, for angels, and for the Gods; for intelligent beings to be crowned with glory, immortality, and eternal lives. In fact, it is the thread which runs from the beginning to the end … from eternity to eternity."[19]

Mankind has been casual with the verb "to marry," such as "marrying" two parts hydrogen and one part oxygen to get water. More or less harmless. But joining two people of the same sex in matrimony fractures the original ideal and can only have the adversary as its source. And that is not harmless.

From *The Family: A Proclamation to the World*, another unequivocal statement:

"Marriage between man and woman is essential to [God's] eternal plan."

Though the world may split marriage into two or even more types, marriage **under God's law** remains sacred. To change, alter, substitute or multiply its definition is to cheapen it. How can it be otherwise? Joining two people of the same gender together in "marriage" is ,an affront to God, one He never intended and will never accept.

President Gordon B. Hinckley:

"Some portray legalization of so-called same-sex marriage as a civil right. This is not a matter of civil rights; it is a matter of morality. Others question our constitutional right as a church to raise our voice on an issue that is of critical importance to the future of the family. We believe that defending this sacred institution by working to preserve traditional marriage lies clearly within our religious and constitutional prerogatives. Indeed, we are compelled by our doctrine to speak out."[20]

It was amazing after the U.S. Supreme Court's 2015 *Obergefell* decision legalizing same-sex marriage that a few members of the Church actually thought it would lead to same-sex temple marriages.

That the United States and many nations have legalized same-sex marriage according to man's laws does not mean that marriage under God's law ceases to be sacred, or that it somehow need not be honored.

> "A society which permits anything will eventually lose everything."
> – Neal A. Maxwell

Family: Fracture Unity

Nothing tells us about the family as succinctly as the brilliant 1995 *Proclamation on the Family.* Note these key points:

- "The family is **ordained of God**."

- "Children are entitled to birth within the **bonds of matrimony**."

- They are "to be reared by a father and a mother who **honor marital vows** with complete fidelity."

- "Happiness in family life is most likely to be achieved when founded upon the **teachings of the Lord Jesus Christ**."

- "**By divine design**, fathers are to **preside** over their families in love and righteousness and are responsible to **provide** the necessities of life and **protection** for their families."

191

- Also **by divine design**, "Mothers are **primarily** responsible for the **nurture** of their children."

- "In these sacred responsibilities, fathers and mothers are obligated to help one another as **equal partners**."

- "We call upon responsible citizens and officers of government everywhere to … strengthen the **family as the fundamental unit of society**."

It would be difficult to find any other statement written by man that exceeds the truth and power of those key points.

Up against such obvious truths, Satan's attack on the family boils down to three tools:

> "The adversary has targeted women and has painted motherhood as a dead-end road of drudgery. He has targeted men and has painted fatherhood as unimportant and fidelity as 'old-school.'"
>
> – Quentin L. Cook

Commonize the word. A team, close friends, colleagues at work, any group can be called, in today's common usage, a family – the family of mankind, the football-fan family, the corporate family, the government family, and so on. Even pets. It is applied to so many things that its true meaning is shunted to the sidelines along with the clarity of its role in the eternities.

Disrupt the actual. While death is an obvious disrupter of families, the more damaging version is divorce, especially separation triggered by infidelity. It also pops up when we fail to recognize that each gender brings its own unique strengths to the family. Much as fathers and mothers are to share duties and work together, **men and women are not fungible**, particularly as such traits may relate to rearing children. When divinely appointed roles are subverted by the wiles of the adversary, family power to progress is crippled.

Vulgarize the sacred. The *Family Proclamation* states, "We declare the means by which mortal life is created to be divinely appointed." Because Satan will never have a mortal body and the procreative powers to become a father, he reduces the sublime act of procreation to vulgarities.

Religion: Cut the Vocab

Author Steve Dunn Hanson put it this way:

"There are those in our increasingly secular world who are attempting to redefine morality. … [T]heir *new* righteousness, their rubric, is *tolerance* – the apparent wholesale acceptance of culture-bending aberrations. … The secularist brand of tolerance is literally the de-religionizing of our society; scrubbing out the Divine and mocking individual eternal potential …."[21]

De-religionizing. Hanson's word captures what's happening today – secularists are working to eliminate or, at a minimum, delegitimize religion.

Mark Davies, Professor of Linguistics at BYU, created a system that counts how frequently words are used in news articles over time. The Time magazine collection from 1923 to 2006 comes from 275,000 articles, numbers over 100 million words, and "serves as a great resource to examine change in American English during this time period."[22]

Look what has happened with religious words in the last half of the 20th century into the first few years of this.

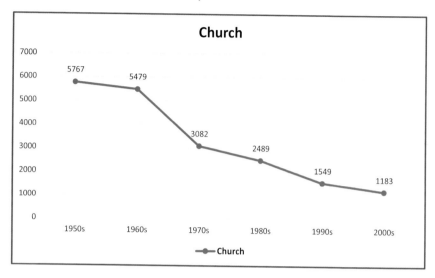

These obviously religious words are in decline:

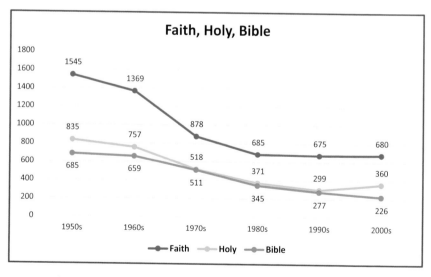

Use of the word *scripture* had a peak in the 1960s but is now back where it was in the 1950s — only 64 mentions.

The religion-designated destinations:

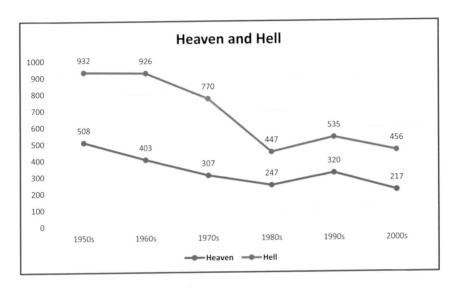

Sin and its source:

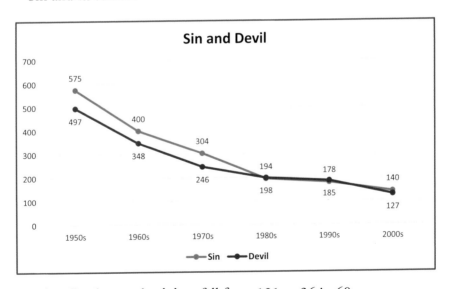

Relatedly, the word *adultery* fell from 121 to 36 in 60 years.

As for similar concepts:

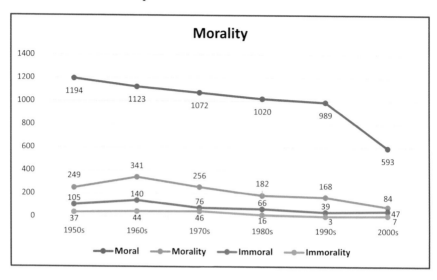

Interesting that we are more comfortable talking adjectives than nouns. Adjectives get more mentions than their corresponding concepts.

Now the counterpart cleansing:

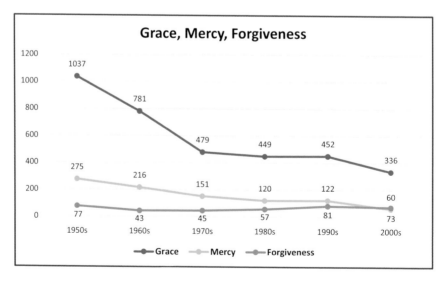

Repentance as a concept has never been a common word, moving from a high of 28 in its best decade to 7 mentions in the first years of this century.

Note here the surge of the word *gay* since 1990:

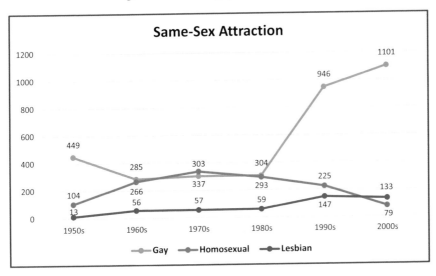

And very few are thinking about the event available today and the one we'll all enjoy someday:

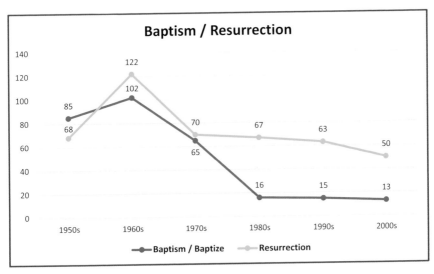

The bottom line: **We're not speaking the language of religion, why should we expect people to be interested in it, let alone guided by it?** Religious words being shunned in our news reports and conversations, why be surprised that certain forces feel emboldened to prohibit religion itself from the public square?

Dennis Prager notes, "When a woman is pregnant and wants to give birth, no one asks her, no matter how early in the pregnancy, 'So, how's the fetus doing?' We only use the term 'fetus' when we plan to destroy it. Otherwise we use 'baby' from the first day of pregnancy."[23]

In contrast, pro-abortion National Public Radio policy states: "The term 'unborn' implies that there is a baby inside a pregnant woman, not a fetus. Babies are not babies until they are born. They're fetuses." [24]

Freedom of Religion

The original meaning of the first of five mentioned freedoms in the First Amendment – "Congress shall make no law respecting an establishment of religion, or prohibiting the free exercise thereof ..." – is under attack and a rising weapon is the **code game**.

The word "code" in itself suggests a secret – some people are in on it, others not. The phrase "code word" thus implies a sinister activity hidden from the public. One doesn't have to prove a connection and that's the beauty of the tactic. The mere use of "code word" implies a person has uncovered a secret and justifies an attack on an opponent with whatever vile descriptions he chooses.

To illustrate our present situation, consider this statement from Martin Castro, Chairman of U.S. Commission on Civil Rights:

"The phrases 'religious liberty' and 'religious freedom' will stand for nothing except hypocrisy so long as they remain code words for discrimination, intolerance, racism, sexism, homophobia, Islamophobia, Christian supremacy or any form of intolerance."

He's playing the code game. His use of the word "remain" is a clever way to imply *religious freedom* has long been the cover for intolerance and other bads.

I would ask Mr. Castro, "Where is the strong evidence that *religious freedom* is a code word for all the negatives you attach to it?" One can always find someone who claims allegiance to a value but has acted contrary; they're called data outliers for a reason. But to claim they represent the totality of those holding the value – to blithely accept tortured and stretched connections based on the actions, if any, of small minorities of the religious community – is despicable.

Religious freedom will continue to be a prime battle-ground in two theaters – the courtroom and the public square. While we may think the phrase's meaning is obvious, as indeed it has been for centuries, secularists use it as code for imposing Christian faith on others. They ridicule it as detrimental rubbish, claim its leaders are bathed in masculine toxicity, and its followers are bigoted, even connected to the Ku Klux Klan. Feeling justified in such distorted views, secularists conclude that freedom to practice it must be eliminated.

> "Freedom to believe in private and to exercise belief and speech in the public square are essential to protecting unalienable rights."
>
> – Quentin L. Cook

"Our government is succumbing to pressure to distance itself from God and religion," warns President M. Russell Ballard. "Consequently, the government is discovering that it is incapable of contending with people who are increasingly 'unbridled by morality and religion.'"

Further evidence comes from the ACLU which claims that religion is being used by believers to discriminate against and harm others.

Just as with natural unequal outcomes, when religious beliefs are seen as villainous discrimination, and charges of hate speech and bigotry add fuel, there is no violation of liberty that some court of law will not justify. Our government in the future may not be the guarantor of religious freedom the Constitution requires.

Elder Neal A. Maxwell predicted: "We shall see in our time a maximum ... effort ... to establish irreligion as the state religion. ... This new irreligious imperialism [will seek] to disallow certain ... opinions simply because those opinions grow out of religious convictions."[25]

ෆ

"The faithful use of our agency depends upon
our having religious freedom."

– Robert D. Hales

Chapter 16

Centralization
The Fire That Warms
Can Also Destroy

"Democracy can hardly be expected to flourish
in societies where political and economic power
is being progressively concentrated and centralized."
— Aldous Huxley

Combining powers for efficiency and teamwork is one thing.
Centralization of power is a different matter.

Societies create rules by which its members live.

Societies over time centralize
the authority to administer those rules.

Reasonable centralization respects
individual agency and facilitates efficiency.

Beyond that modicum, however,
centralized power attracts those who seek it
for pride, dominion, fame, and gain.

Though more societies try to control power
through separation, division, and specific
enumeration, the natural inclination for
power to become concentrated continues.

Satan wants full centralization
because concentrated power is easier to
subvert than disseminated power.

The patron saint of centralized government "thought the conditions of modern times demanded that government power be <u>unified</u> rather than fragmented and checked. His great confidence in the wisdom of science and benevolence of expert administrators led him to the view that <u>the founders' worries about concentrated power were obsolete</u>. He exhibited the combination of love for power and unbounded paternalism that is the hallmark of the administrative state today. [He wrote] 'If I saw my way to it as a practical politician, I should be willing to go farther and <u>superintend every man's use of his chance</u>.'"[1]

Got that? Superintend every man's use of his chance – **be the supervisor of every man's agency**. Control, control, control. And if there's any doubt, he further wrote, "Men are as clay in the hands of the consummate leader" and "Resistance is left to the minority, and such as will not be convinced are crushed."[2]

Agency a mere nicety and people clay to be molded. Thanks, Woodrow Wilson.

Ꮤ

Power seekers don't want to climb to the top of their power pyramid only to find themselves in competition with neighboring pyramids. Therefore the urge to centralize the system so one need only climb one pyramid to reach supremacy.

Consider how the danger unfolds:

- Concentration is by definition the opposite of separation. Centralization downplays, even disregards, the separation and division of power specified by the Constitution.

- It encourages bigger government. Fewer people wielding power is intoxicating.

- As local voices wane and a central voice dominates, freedom shrinks.

- Concentrated power is a more visible power and is intimidating. We begin to fear being restricted or fined.

- Advocates of centralization want conformity and work to keep individuals in line. We find we have fewer choices, which in turn weakens agency.

- Centralization's curtailment of freedoms takes a toll on motivation and innovation. We become less sure we'll enjoy the fruits of our labor.

- Less voluntary cooperation results in less productivity of the free market.

"Our minds tell us, and history confirms," explained Milton Friedman, "that **the great threat to freedom is the concentration of power.** Government is necessary to preserve our freedom, it is an instrument through which we can exercise our freedom; yet by concentrating power in political hands, it is also a threat to freedom."

> Rulers look down.
> Leaders look forward.

He added: "Even though the men who wield this power initially be of good will and even though they be not corrupted by the power they exercise, the **power will both attract and form men of a different stamp.**"[3]

What began as a need for efficiency became a convenient path to power for "men of a different stamp," and Washington today brims with them.

Centralization Aids Satan's Plan

As mentioned earlier, the problem is how to give a leader enough power to accomplish good but not so much that he becomes a tyrant. The solution is demonstrated in the U.S. Constitution where power is separated, divided, and enumerated. In other words, power is decentralized so that a critical mass sufficient to dominate is never found in the hands of one or a few.

Satan hates this. He does not want a multiple-viewpoint, robust-debate, balanced system. The last thing he wants is people who think, consider choices, make decisions, act, learn, progress, and develop divine attributes. The fewer decisions you get to make, the better for him.

His recipe is simple. **Centralized power concentrated among a few is easier to usurp than disseminated power.** One need only persuade a few big kahunas in Washington or other single location rather than work on every person who holds a measure of power in multiple geographic areas.

> "The centralization of power in Washington, which nearly all members of Congress deplore in their speech and then support by their votes, steadily increases."
>
> – Calvin Coolidge

Human nature helps the process. Those who would pull our strings do not like competition from other string pullers. Each string puller therefore works to accrue and consolidate as much power as possible not only for the satisfying joy of wielding it over the general population, but also to relegate competition into subordinate roles. The clear example is federal officers dominating state and local officials.

President Ezra Taft Benson saw it over 50 years ago:

"Ever-increasing centralization of power in the federal government in Washington, D.C. is reducing our local and state governments to **virtual federal field offices while weakening individual initiative, enterprise and character.**"[4]

The intensity of the division now expands beyond the <u>political</u> sphere and seeps into the fiber of our <u>culture</u> as average citizens are disparaged as ignorant deplorables in flyover country. Legitimate differences of opinion morph into hatred and Washington's power hungry unleash ever-increasing rules to smother and wear down the American people.

The Turning Point

Before one has power to command obedience, how does he persuade others to centralize power on himself? There comes a hinge-point in the centralization process where people tire of voluntary teamwork and yearn for someone to pull people together and really get things rolling. I maintain the oft-overlooked ingredient in the recipe to accelerate centralization to full bloom is flattery – sympathetic promising words on the tongue of a charismatic personality.

Every villain in the Book of Mormon seeking power was facile with words and excelled at flattery. Every one of them. To name a few:

Sherem was "learned, that he had a **perfect knowledge of the language** of the people; wherefore, he could use much flattery ..."[5]

Korihor demonstrated his power of language in an argument with Alma, who said it is better that Korihor be lost than souls be brought down to destruction "by thy lying and by thy **flattering words** ..."[6]

Nehor was large and noted for his strength, but he had to be glib because "many did believe on his words"[7] which ran opposite to the prophets.

King Noah's people "became idolatrous, because they were deceived by the vain and flattering words of the king …"[8]

Amalickiah, the villain of choice in king-men days, was "a man of cunning device and a man of many **flattering words** …"[9]

Even Alma the Younger, in his pre-angel-appearance days, "was a man of **many words**, and did speak much flattery to the people …"[10]

And check out Giddianhi's letter to Lachoneus[11] – smooth and insidious flattery in action.

There must be a reason 15 such examples are given in the Book of Mormon. The Lord warns against "the wise, and the learned, … who are puffed up because of their learning"[12] because He knows where it can lead.

Flattery, excessive praise from **motives of self interest**, requires and builds on class distinctions – a shared sense of us versus them. The flatterer has to identify an enemy, usually the rich or those in power – the convenient "they," along these lines …

You deserve better. "They" are preventing you from obtaining what is rightly yours. "They" hate you. It's "their" fault you are suffering. Support me and I will give you power. I will make you rulers over "them."

Flattery can be sharpened by promising to tax the rich and give the persuadees the money. So doing, opportunistic schmoozers centralize power in themselves.

Warning Signs of Power Centralization

Failure to put individual agency at the top of society's priorities has always led, and will always lead, to corruption and abuse of power – gradually, insidiously, and then a surge. What are the early warning signals of unwelcome centralization?

- A noticeable reduction of choices.

- Excessive emphasis on efficiency; comments that centralized power will be more efficient than disseminated power.

- Increased demand for experts, implicitly meaning others who are smarter than those presently assembled.

- An imbalance between a necessary headquarters and a system for inputs from constituents who may not live close to those headquarters.

- Geographic location becomes less a factor of convenience and more a perceived pool of wisdom: "Let Washington solve it."

- Unwarranted isolation of decision makers from those they represent; laborious procedures for interaction.

- Zealous enforcement of rules; slavish adherence to the letter of the law over common sense.

- Overstepping of authority, an increase in bossy people exerting more control than necessary.

- Failure to delegate down; ignoring the ideal that a problem should be solved at the level closest to the problem.

- Increased references to a "living Constitution" – that the principles of yesteryear don't apply in today's world.

- Worship of the mean; stigmatizing differences for the goal of equal outcomes.

- Increasing entitlements that weaken resistance to power-centralizing efforts.

- Homogenization: the preaching of diversity but the practice of lock-step conformity.

- Undue attention to those who claim to be victims; jealousy of the success of others.

All of these lead to the centralization of power that is Satan's counterfeit of how God would have us use it.

> "There's very little government can do as efficiently and economically as the people can do for themselves."
>
> – Ronald Reagan

"The greatest advances of civilization," said Milton Friedman, "whether in architecture or painting, in science and literature, in industry or agriculture, have never come from centralized government."

Church Decentralization – The Counter Example

So how does the Church differ from legislatures and government bureaucracies? Here are a few critical differences:

- The Church does not incur long-term debt. Income and expenditures balance out each year.

- We work on a pay-as-you-go basis. We don't leave the bill for someone else.

- The Church reverses the government pattern. Instead of spending the next generation's money for today's members, it uses today's money for the benefit of both today's and tomorrow's members.

- We act together and take responsibilities for ourselves and for our roles, whatever they may be. We periodically affirm our support for our leaders' actions.

- Any deferred consequences onto future generations are designed to be positive ones.

- We try to solve problems at the levels closest to the problems. Power is diffused throughout the organization. A central authority establishes guidelines and principles; leaders and members at the local level solve the problems closest to them.

- We trust members to learn correct principles and to govern themselves. Stacks of rules and regulations are unknown in the Church.

While man's history shows that concentrated power in a society is almost always detrimental to its citizens, God has concentrated power but shares it and everyone benefits. Counter-intuitive as it might sound, He actually gains more power because as His children progress, they honor Him – glory and honor being synonymous with power.[13]

Not that long ago, all missionaries were interviewed for worthiness by an apostle. It was a special experience for me to have been interviewed by then-Elder Harold B. Lee. That decision authority has now been decentralized down to stake presidents.

Following important organizational changes over the years, "the stake assumed its role as the major governing unit **between** the wards and Church headquarters. Stakes were now expected to have responsibility for every person and every program within their boundaries. Decentralization by the transference of more priesthood responsibility to the stakes has continued as Church membership has expanded."[14]

President Hinckley specifically used the key word in 1995: "As the work grows across the world it has become necessary to **decentralize administrative authority to keep General Authorities closer to the people.**"

This policy will expand to other Church activities because decentralization aligns with the way God disseminates his gifts of power. Just as **"it is not meet"** that God commands in all things,[15] it is not meet that his prophets, seers and revelators make every decision.

The Church is *vertical* for authority and guiding principles and *horizontal* for individual latitude and the *application* of authority. We become unified without being centralized.

In short, decentralization of power is the *essence* of the U.S. Constitution that was *established* by God. It therefore follows that **man's centralization of power runs contrary to God's ways.**

This trend will become even more salient and threatening as more nation-states entertain the idea of ceding powers to supra-national courts and legislative bodies – globalism.

೧

"No plan of centralization has ever been adopted
which did not result in bureaucracy, tyranny,
inflexibility, reaction, and decline."
– Calvin Coolidge

Chapter 17

Statism
Imagine a Rule for Everything

"If [God] undertook to tell us each time
what we were to do in every detail … [it] would virtually
destroy the free agency of man, the foundation stone
upon which all of our existence is built."

– J. Reuben Clark

"[King George III] has erected a Multitude of new Offices,
and sent hither Swarms of Officers to harass our People,
and eat out their Substance."

– Declaration of Independence

Societies organize and administer laws
for safety, well-being, and survival.

People want better societies, but disagree about methods.

One method is to <u>improve self</u> – let agency work
so man will act, learn from consequences, and
create a self-governing society with minimum rules.

Another method is to <u>control others</u> –
write and enforce regulations to prevent
every possible mistake in human behavior.

Administrative entities are necessary,
but governments have no natural inhibiting
mechanisms to control their own growth.

Excessive bureaucracy violates
the gift of individual agency:

- It assumes people need to be more controlled
  and therefore more rules are written that
  restrict choices and freedom;

- It fosters a rule-obedient instead of an
  action-responsible society and thus interferes
  with responsibility and accountability;

- It strives for a perfect society by attempting
  to prevent all mistakes and thus curtails
  individual learning and progress;

- It produces an authoritarian and
  over-protective society thus under-cutting
  the role of positive-friction opposition.

And agency suffers.

It is a crime in the United States of America to … consult with a known pirate, let your pet make a noise that scares wildlife in a national park, injure a government-owned lamp, sell diced onions formed as onion rings without saying so, take home milk from a quarantined giraffe, skydive while drunk, or hunt pigeons with a machine gun.[1]

In some states you cannot … dance to the national anthem, wrestle a bear, sell your children, or use a drone to hunt birds. In other states, cannibalism is outlawed and cows have the right-of-way on highways.[2] In Oregon, the government owns the rain and you must have a permit to collect it and hold it, even on your own private property.

In certain cities you cannot … spit on a road, swear while driving, build a nuclear weapon, eat fried chicken with a fork, or keep a skunk as a pet. Further, your kids cannot throw snowballs.[3] Lemonade stands? A chapter by itself.

We're drowning in silly rules.

☙

"[T]he sovereign extends its arms over society …
with a network of petty regulations, complicated, minute,
and uniform …. It does not break wills but softens them …
it does not tyrannize, it hinders, compromises, enervates,
extinguishes, dazes, and finally reduces each nation to
nothing more than a herd of timid and industrious animals
of which the government is the shepherd."[4]
– Alexis de Tocqueville

And eventually not even industrious.

Numerous books have been written about burgeoning government bureaucracy often referred to as the Deep State, the administrative state, the fourth branch of government – statism. We can only touch on a fraction of the juicy mess, so here are a few insights from the perspective of how statism impacts agency.

The Setting

The Appeal

The Game

The Jargon

The Family

The Damage

The Danger

The Setting – Relentless Growth

In 1961, President John F. Kennedy oversaw 450 political and career executives who occupied 17 bureaucratic layers at the top of government. Today the president oversees more than 3000 executives in 63 layers.[5] For every one of those people Kennedy supervised, we now have a full agency – 450 major agencies and numerous offices, institutes, bureaus, and centers under them.[6] Not counting the military or postal service employees, we have 2.1 million federal government workers. The federal government is the nation's largest single employer.[7]

> Government is not too big? Then why, when Washington is hit with a snowstorm, does it tell "non-essential federal workers" to stay home?

216

And look what they've produced.

As of January 2019, the *Code of Federal Regulations*, the archive of all federal rules, contains over 185,000 pages of rules (many per page) derived from thousands of pages of the *Federal Register*, the government's "diary." Stack those pages one upon the other and the pile would be the height of a six-story building. That there were less than 23,000 such pages in 1960 (a little less than seven feet tall) shows the explosive growth of government's obsessive urge to control all human behavior.[8]

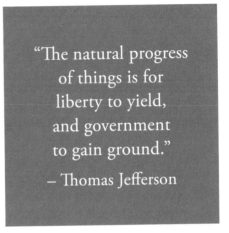

"The natural progress of things is for liberty to yield, and government to gain ground."

– Thomas Jefferson

That America is subject to more than 185,000 pages of rules does not suggest a light sprinkling of do's and don'ts. The Jewish people of the Savior's time were lucky – they only had 613 rules they had to follow.

Obesity isn't limited to people.

The Appeal – Unchecked Power

When centralization met intellectualism, the die was cast.

Given the choice between bureaucracy and business, few intellectuals choose the latter. The market economy does not reward intellectuals "according to their own estimation of their obvious social worth," so numerous intellectuals gravitate toward power and they love the idea of a hierarchy apart from the free market, one that will worship their IQs.

Today intellectuals "play leading roles in the bureaucracies of the state, as advisors, experts, and administrators, and increasing the power of the state means increasing the power of the intellectuals" – "a place in the sun, in which their cash rewards are almost certainly higher, and in which power rewards are undoubtedly higher."[9]

Why would people who think they are smart not be attracted to take jobs where they have power to tell others what to do? The chance to indulge their inner bully is an obvious appeal of Deep State employment, but other perks entice as well:

- They are not elected and are not answerable to the voters.

- It is very difficult to fire them.

- Congress has oversight responsibility on their activities, but finds it difficult to ride herd. They're basically on their own.

- If they write rules that stir a fuss, it's easy to deny authorship. They tell investigators it was done by committee or they don't know who did it.

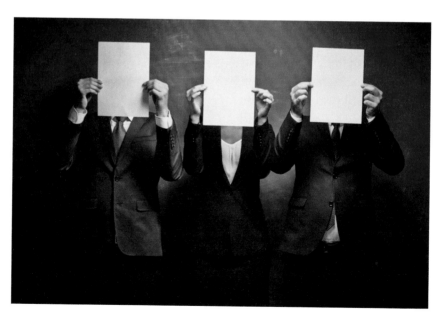

- They receive higher pay compared to the private sector.

- Unless they are in the higher ranks, they are invisible.

- For all practical purposes, they have power without being accountable.

The motives of such people "have nothing to do with the welfare of other people," writes Thomas Sowell. "Instead, they have two related goals – to establish themselves as morally and intellectually superior to the rather distasteful population of common people, and to **gather as much power as possible to tell those distasteful common people how they must live their lives.**"[10]

"A civil servant who has forgotten how to be civil," counseled Elder Neal A. Maxwell, "may have some sway now in the procurement division of a vast government direction, but he is headed in just the opposite developmental direction needed for sway in the next world. … [And] the civic leader whose thirst for recognition causes him to do things to be seen of men has his reward."[11]

> "I believe there are more instances of the abridgement of the freedom of the people by gradual and silent encroachments of those in power than by violent and sudden usurpations."
>
> – James Madison

The attitude plays out at all levels of government. In Santa Barbara, California in 2018, for example, a city councilman acknowledged the end goal: "Unfortunately, common sense is just not common. We have to regulate every aspect of people's lives."

Think about it. Every aspect?! Those who subscribe to such a philosophy restrict your agency. You are not allowed to freely choose,

> "Sometimes your freedom is not taken away at gunpoint but instead is done one piece of paper at a time, one seemingly meaningless rule at a time, one small silencing at a time."
>
> – Armando Valladares, anti-Castro activist

experience, and learn. You are controlled by the rules and regulations. Beyond the obvious need to set reasonable rules to protect life and property, such activism quickly becomes unrighteous dominion.

With the attitude that government has the right to regulate every aspect of our lives, the birth of rule-happy bureaucracies was inevitable. Sovereignty of the people slides closer to cliff's edge.

The Game – Find Problems But Don't Solve Them

If you work in the private sector, you are successful if people buy your product or service and you make a profit. If you work in the public sector, on the other hand, the **markers of success are the size of your budget and how many people are under you – neither of which depends on the customer.**

If government services were dependent upon free-will purchases, would we hire others to tell us what we can and cannot do? Hardly. Only services that protect us against foreign enemies, maintain domestic tranquility, and help us adjudicate our differences would be freely purchased.

Therefore, bureaucrats have to sell their services some other way. A favorite is to build upon the false sense of togetherness in the phrase "Government is what we do together" to foist the conclusion that every problem has a government solution.[12] Once they get people looking to government for answers, all they have to do is supply the problems.

But not the solutions.

Here's why. To be successful, a bureaucrat must find a problem and write rules and regulations that address it. But if he solves the problem, public employee jobs could be lost, including his. Therefore the technique is to burrow deeper into Americans' daily lives to find, or invent, problems that justify the agency's existence and help it grow, and **subject the problem to a process rather than a solution.**

One columnist observed, "…politicians require a steady stream of crises from which they can purport to save us"[13] – the saving, of course, coming in the form of handing over more money, power, and freedom to the state. Another observer concluded that bureaucracies never want to solve problems, but to *manage* them; their success is, perversely but directly, a function of inefficiency.[14]

The bureaucrat's mindset: find a problem, protect it, study it, complicate it, stretch it out, hold conferences, do research, write rules, dream up alphabet-soup acronyms, monitor, regulate, administer and maintain the problem, but whatever you do don't solve the hummer or we'll all be peddling apples and pencils.

> Bureaucrats don't care what the customer thinks.

> "You will never understand bureaucracies until you understand that for bureaucrats procedure is everything and outcomes are nothing."
>
> – Thomas Sowell

The Jargon – Vague, Verbose, Voluminous

Most day-to-day regulations we must obey were not written by elected lawmakers.

The process is simple. Congress passes what is in reality a verbose wish list – the Clean Air Act, the Clean Water Act, the Safe Drinking Water Act, the Affordable Care Act, etc. – and empowers administrative agencies to fill in the details. Clear definitions are often missing, verbiage is vague and open to interpretation, congressional oversight of the final rules virtually non-existent.

The verbosity of average legislation doesn't help and some laws are hardly read before Congress votes on them. As House Speaker Nancy Pelosi famously said of the Affordable Care Act in 2010, "We have to pass the bill so that you can find out what's in it."[15]

James Madison warned that even laws made by chosen representatives "will be of little avail to the people ... if the laws be so voluminous that they cannot be read, or so incoherent that they cannot be understood."[16]

Vague, voluminous, verbose verbiage allows bureaucrats to specify details however they desire. Take the Clean Water Act. The EPA interpreted it so government could control "any creek, muddy farm field, ditch or prairie pothole located within a 'significant nexus' of a navigable waterway."[17] And what is a "significant nexus"? Anything that imaginative statists define it to be. After all, bureaucrats themselves are not a whit behind Congress when it comes to vague verbiage. Vagueness affords latitude to interpret meaning and maximize power.

Unelected, unaccountable agency apparatchiks also use *guidance letters* to circumvent judicial and legislative review. These are flat-out decrees not based on anything Congress has written nor handled through the established rule-making process. "The most notorious example is the Education Department's 2011 'Dear Colleague' letter which mandated that universities use a lower burden of proof in sexual-misconduct investigations."[18] Who gave them the authority to "mandate" such a major change in due-process law? No one; they took it upon themselves.

To exercise power, the administrative state stretches, extends, and **manipulates legislative intent**.

The Family – Keep It Within

Bureaucracy's power game doesn't end with writing words on parchment. Columbia Law Professor Philip Hamburger described it this way:

"Sometimes called the regulatory state or the deep state, it is a government within the government, run by the president and the dozens of federal agencies that assume powers once claimed only by kings. In place of royal decrees, they issue rules and send out "guidance" letters …. Unelected bureaucrats not only write their own laws, they also interpret these laws and enforce them in their own courts with their own judges. All this is in blatant violation of the Constitution …."[19]

Professor Hamburger then detailed how the abusive administrative state ignores the separation-of-power principle and hijacks judicial, legislative, and executive functions to itself. Using the Federal Trade Commission as an example, the adjacent diagram illustrates Hamburger's description of typical enforcement activities of federal agencies.

So, people who receive their paycheck from the *executive* branch use *legislative* powers to write laws, use *judicial* powers to judge and assess fines on those who break them, and again use *executive* powers to collect the fines. And the agency keeps the money, thus intensifying the incentive to write even more rules.

In a way, the administrative state – insular, tight, closed to outsiders – is its own priestcraft religion. The three-pound god reigns; the Federal Register is scripture; bureaucrats are priests who impose religious doctrine; and taxation and penalties provide the funds without passing the plate.

Gary Lawson of Boston University School of Law concludes:

"The modern administrative state is not merely unconstitutional; **it is anti-constitutional**. The Constitution was designed specifically to prevent the emergence of the kinds of institutions that characterize the modern administrative state. … The destruction of this principle of separation of powers is perhaps the crowning jewel of the modern administrative revolution."[20]

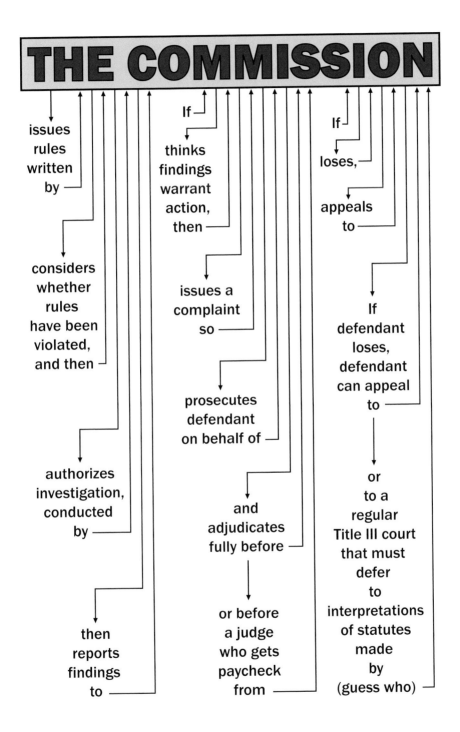

THE COMMISSION

issues
rules
written
by ——

considers
whether
rules
have been
violated,
and then ⌐

authorizes
investigation,
conducted
by ——

then
reports
findings
to ——

If ⌐
thinks
findings
warrant
action,
then ——

issues a
complaint
so ——

prosecutes
defendant
on behalf of ⌐

and
adjudicates
fully before ⌐

or before
a judge
who gets
paycheck
from ——

If ⌐
loses, ——

appeals
to ——

If
defendant
loses,
defendant
can appeal
to ——

or
to a
regular
Title III court
that must
defer
to
interpretations
of statutes
made
by
(guess who) ⌐

The Damage – Hits on Agency

Consider five impacts from the growth of statism.

First, <u>limits freedom</u>. No human activity exists that one agency or another has not placed under its umbrella to monitor, administer, and if necessary bend to its will. Because the administrative state believes people cannot be trusted to run their own lives, rules must govern every possible human activity. But as Ronald Reagan put it, "Man is not free unless government is limited. … As government expands, liberty contracts."[21]

> Which kingdom
> of heaven will have
> the fewest rules?

Second, <u>discourages action and risks</u>. Instead of agency's robust trial-and-error experiments to assess the success of an idea, excessive government smothers ingenuity and produces caution. The willingness to act and take risks goes down because the probability of success is harder to envision in a cluttered world of rules.

As more control is ceded to the ambitious intellectual nobility squirreled away in sprawling bureaucracies, people become sheeple intimidated into inaction.

Why should a would-be entrepreneur, willing to take normal risks associated with research and development, risk offending some unseen martinet looking to flex his "thou shalt not" prerogatives and fine him for violating some obscure regulation?

Third, <u>stifles innovation and progress</u>. Milton Friedman observed:

> "The world runs on people pursuing their self interests. The great achievements of civilization have not come from government bureaus. Einstein didn't construct his theory

under order from a bureaucrat. Henry Ford didn't revolutionize the automobile industry that way."

How many innovative and creative entrepreneurs seek government jobs? Few. Dr. Tom Stossel, professor emeritus at Harvard Medical School, notes as an example:

"The private economy, not the government, actually discovers and develops most of the insights and products that advance health."

Fourth, <u>cuts experience and learning</u>. We all want to prevent mistakes that *significantly* harm others, but is it wise to eliminate all mistakes? Interfering with freedom of action and interrupting the law of consequences might reduce friction in society, but would that be wise? After all, no friction, no progress.

We may be approaching a point where stifling rules overwhelm and deprive people of opportunities to learn from the bumps of life. Is it really government's role to monitor our weight and dictate what we eat?

Agency works best when people are left to learn from their own mistakes, and in the process perhaps generate friction for others to use.

> "The market gives people what the people want, instead of what other people think they ought to want. At the bottom of many criticisms of the market economy is really lack of belief in freedom itself."[22]
>
> – Milton Friedman

Fifth, <u>abets corruption</u>. Growth of the administrative state makes it difficult to terminate unproductive employees (a member of my local school board estimates it costs $300,000 to fire one public school

> "Let us, by exercising our privileges under the Constitution … feel free to plan and to reap without the handicap of bureaucratic interference."
>
> – David O. McKay

teacher), insulates agencies that forget who their masters are, fosters an us-versus-them culture and a "circle the wagons" mentality when an agency comes under fire. And they are oblivious about money. After all, they rationalize, even $100 million dollars in expenses only costs each American thirty cents.

Statism leads to inefficient and dysfunctional government prone to be hijacked by special interests. Senate Leader Mitch McConnell:

"Over the past several decades, the same public employees who've arrogated vast powers to themselves have conspired with their patrons in Congress to expand those powers even more, and to endlessly increase the budgets that finance them."[23]

That corruption, government overreach, and crony capitalism are byproducts should come as no surprise. In short, **government coercion violates agency and therefore harms freedom, creativity, innovation, production, and progress.**

And if cultural corruption leads to corruption of law as established by the voice of the people, we read in Helaman the looming consequence:

… they saw that their laws had become corrupted, and … they who chose evil were more numerous than they who chose good, therefore they were ripening for destruction, for the laws had become corrupted.[24]

The Danger – A Rule-Driven Morality

Beyond the visible damage lurks **the real danger: people will cease to be guided by moral principles.**

Recalling insights triggered by a conversation with a Marxist economist from China, Harvard professor Clayton Christensen reaffirmed how democracy and prosperity depend upon the **voluntary obedience to the unenforceable** laws of morality, and such are instilled in us through religion, not culture.[25] That is, we must be **self-governing** based on moral principles rather than **other-governed** based on countless picky rules. Bloated bureaucracies downgrade moral principles and so doing can change one's outlook on life.

Reasonable rules and regulations are necessary for an orderly society – the "cannots" such as traffic rules and the "musts" such as taxes. But as bureaucrats expand their territory beyond the necessary minimum, more regulations become permissions (things citizens "may do") or commands (things a citizen "must do"). More things to control our lives.

> While Joseph Smith said, "I teach them correct principles and they govern themselves," bureaucrats yammer, "Tell them the rules and we'll govern them ourselves."

"Since it lacks the self-control apparatus that is a major part of religion," Dennis Prager observes, "the Left passes more and more laws to control people. That is why there is a **direct link between the decline in Judeo-Christian religion and the increase in governmental laws controlling human behavior.**"[26]

Although there's not enough paper in the world to write a rule for every possible behavior under every possible condition, power elites try their best and people chafe at the weight of expanding regulations. But let's say such a tome of rules existed. Would life be better? No. It would be frozen. Even as it is today, people forced to function at a look-over-your-shoulder micro level forget overarching principles and rationalize their behavior. They seek loopholes, work around details, massage words, and argue the picky. They game the system.

> "Unless bureaucracy is constantly resisted it breaks down representative government and overwhelms democracy. It is the one element in our institutions that sets up the pretense of having authority over everybody and being responsible to nobody."[27]
>
> – Calvin Coolidge

As regulations grow, attention shifts from *traditional morality* ("Is it right or wrong?") to *moral relativism* and picky diktats ("Is there a rule against it?"). And even if there is a rule against it, violators rationalize "It's okay as long as I don't get caught" or "If I get caught, the punishment isn't that bad." (An example of the latter is California's Proposition 47 downgrading penalties for shoplifting less than $950 of merchandise. Guess what's happening in San Francisco.[28])

Too many people today think governing behavior is someone else's problem. Sadly, there are many who are only too happy to govern other people's behavior, or enjoy the power of trying. **The more such mini-bosses exercise power with dump-loads of regulations, the greater the thinking that it's up to government to govern the individual.**

People thus become less self-governing and the thinking shifts from …

"I will be guided by principles" … to

"It's okay if there is no law against it" … to

"It's okay as long as I don't get caught."

It's the big morph from <u>action-responsible</u> to <u>rule-obedient</u> to <u>rule-dodging</u>.

Once people shift from being self controlled to being externally controlled by others, the world changes. It's as if the man scraps his own conscience and lets government play that role. Responsibility dwindles as regulations pile up, government becomes the final word on all human activity, and we slide toward tyranny.

ℰↃ

"The state will never wither away in a spiritually standardless society. It will simply swell and become more strong, more ominous, and more serious."

– Neal A. Maxwell

Chapter 18

Socialism
The Anti-Agency

"The worst form of inequality is to try
to make unequal things equal."
– Aristotle

"Collectivism is the idea that the individual's life belongs
not to him but to the group or society of which he is merely
a part, that he has no rights, and that he must sacrifice his
values and goals for the group's 'greater good.'"[1]

The very antithesis of agency.

In heaven we were given equality of opportunity
– follow the Savior, keep His commandments,
and return to live with Him and the Father.

Satan, in opposition, preached equality of outcome
– do whatever you want and everyone will still
be saved in the kingdom of God

Today, using agency, people exert unequal efforts,
which necessarily must result in unequal outcomes.

Socialism opposes this fact.

Socialists agitate for equal distribution of wealth
through (1) state control of the means of production,
(2) central planning, and (3) wage and price controls.

Socialism lite consists of aggressive redistribution,
high taxation, numerous regulations, and
a large welfare state.

Whatever the degree of socialism, if unequal efforts
are rewarded with equal outcomes, there is
no justice, no learning, no progress.

Satan agitates for equality of outcomes precisely
because it destroys motivation, justice, and agency.

During an informal get-together, Mikhail Gorbachev asked Prime Minister Margaret Thatcher how goods are priced in the UK economy. She explained costs, labor, demand, overhead, profit margins, etc. only to hear him say, "But somebody must tell them what to charge." Some people, albeit intelligent, just don't get it.

She wrote:

> "We knew what worked: Small government. Low taxes. Sound money. Private property. Enterprise. They are what worked and they always work.

> "We knew too what didn't work – namely, socialism in every shape or form. And how many forms there are! Socialism is like one of those horrible viruses. You no sooner discover a remedy for one version, when it spontaneously evolves into another. ... New slogans: old errors."[2]

Gorbachev's successor Boris Yeltsin once visited Houston's Mission Control and later dropped by a local Randall's supermarket. He was blown away and remarked, "Even the Politburo doesn't have this choice. Not even Mr. Gorbachev."

Yeltsin later wrote:

> "When I saw those shelves crammed with hundreds, thousands of cans, cartons and goods of every possible sort, for the first time I felt quite frankly sick with despair for the Soviet people."[3]

People steeped in socialism are stunned by the free market, whereas some who have always had the free market are stunted by socialism.

☙

The Dangerous Promise of Equal Outcomes

In the following discussion of socialism, keep in mind that labels can be misleading. When the battle is labeled capitalism vs. socialism, people prefer capitalism by a 52-42 margin. When it's labeled free-market economy vs. government-managed economy, the free market wins 64-32.[4]

> Socialism is statism extended to the economy. Its goal is total control.

Historically, socialism raises its head when there has been a failure such as a depression or a war. Socialism's recent barge onto the stage comes from a different spur – the unfettered growth of the administrative state.

The very size of government in America plants the idea among opportunists that as long as government is growing in power, a critical step toward socialism, why not hop on board and enjoy the jolly pursuit of utopia? Thus, despite numerous variations of socialism throughout the world, virtually every one of them a disaster, the naïve and the power hungry have joined forces to provide retooled twists on Marxism, rebranded as progressivism, and claim, "True socialism has never been tried."

> "Have we achieved full socialism?" "Oh, no, things have to get a lot worse."[5]

Here we go again.

Wikipedia lists over 60 types of socialism roaming the world. Weeding out the tweaks and twaddles, seven common features and assumptions of socialism especially clash with agency.

1. Government should control the means of production and prices.

2. Wealth should be equally distributed. If someone has more, it means others have less.

3. Everyone should be equal. No one is better than anyone else, and no one should be left behind. Equality in all things is possible.

4. People have a right to food, housing, jobs, education, and health care. Government should guarantee it.

5. People can be suffused with socialism so they will work as hard for others as they do for themselves.

6. Pursuing gain is greed. People should not possess more money than immediate needs require.

7. Competition for personal gain is evil and must be eliminated. The state must be the sole entrepreneur.

Let's examine each of them.

I. Central Planning and Control Violates the Law of Consequences

"Government is the only thing we all belong to."[6]

Socialists demand the means of production and prices be controlled by society as a whole – in other words, by an unfettered central government. Of course **you may own a business, but what you do with it depends on government's acquiescence** … or direct commands as established by central planning.

Businesses do not freely invite governments
to force business decisions.

But using the force of commands and penalties,
socialist governments <u>control</u> production without
necessarily <u>owning</u> the means of production.

There can be no socialism without force.

Agency is thus violated at its most basic point:
the freedom to choose and to act.

Four things to note. <u>First</u>, in direct contradiction to Joseph Smith's approach, socialism says people cannot be trusted to govern themselves. Socialists are all too eager to show the world they can do a better job … on others, of course.

<u>Second</u>, socialism will never spontaneously appear in a thriving society that follows the principles of agency. The statism trend toward more government feeds socialism. More government means more force, precisely what socialists want because force is critical to bully their ideas into existence.

George Washington observed: "Government is not reason; it is not eloquent; it is force. Like fire, it is a dangerous servant and a fearful master."

Third, ultimate socialism calls for *central ownership* of the means of production. This is too blatant for most people, so activists *insidiously hide behind "control not ownership."*

The deep state pushes for "government control of the economy, while leaving ownership in private hands," Thomas Sowell explained. "That way, politicians get to call the shots but, when their bright ideas lead to disaster, they can always blame those who own businesses in the private sector." They envision themselves as "superior beings pursuing superior ends."

Clever. No need to *own* the actual production facilities; just take over and *direct* the capital that businesses and individuals have traditionally controlled, which in turn prevents scarce resources being guided to their most highly valued use.

> "North Korea could easily learn to feed itself, but the problem is there is only one person who can tell the farmers what to plant, when to plant it, and where to grow it – and he isn't a farmer."[7]

Enemies in World War II, Hitler and Stalin instituted two kinds of socialism. Under communistic socialism in the USSR, the wealthy, such as land-owning kulaks, were exterminated until the state owned everything. Under national socialism in Germany, there was nominal private ownership. Bankers and owners of the means of production were tolerated so long as they conformed to Hitler's decrees and produced wealth for the use of the state.

Apologists today say "their" socialism is different and point to prosperous Scandinavian countries as supposed examples. But based on common definitions, Sweden, Denmark, and Norway are not socialist. Sweden did try socialist ideas years ago, but has moved in the opposite direction by privatizing industries and repealing regulations. The Scandinavian countries some American office-seekers claim are socialist are in fact not planned economies under centralized control. They have private property and private stock exchanges. They are **free-market welfare states** with high taxation rates and significant redistribution, but **the governments do not own, nor excessively control**, the means of production, distribution, or pricing. Living standards as measured by GDP and consumption are higher than in obviously socialist countries, but are 15% lower than we enjoy in the United States.[8]

Fourth, the workplace has always been socialism's favorite hotbed of agitation against the free market. Seeking power, socialists butt into the relationship between employers and employees, and disrupt the natural flow of action-consequence. Consider …

The free market believes in incentives and free-will agreements: If you produce X, I will pay you Y.

Socialism believes if government requires employers to pay Y, workers will produce X.

It's nice to be optimistic, but if workers know they have a guaranteed payment no matter their output, what happens to motivation? While the threat of a consequence (jail) may deter a negative action (robbery), will the guarantee of a government-mandated consequence (money) generate the positive action (product) of a free-will arrangement? Doubtful. You can promise a reward for the right action, but a guarantee no matter the action reveals a poor understanding of motivation.

In the process, a socialism-sympathetic government expands its power and industry loses production. Control a product's price and supply soon evaporates.

"The advantage of a free market is that it allows millions of decision-makers to respond individually to freely determined prices, allocating resources – labor, capital and human ingenuity – in a manner that can't be mimicked by a central plan, however brilliant the central planner."

– Friedrich von Hayek

II. Equal Distribution of Wealth Stifles Effort

Socialists want wealth to be equally distributed. Supposing wealth to be a self-existing commodity, for someone to have more means others have less. So what could be more fair, the thinking goes, than making sure everyone has an equal slice of that miraculous pie and no one goes hungry?

Under socialism, government controls wealth and decides how it shall be allocated.

To facilitate equal distribution and prevent excess accumulation of wealth, government imposes increasingly higher taxes and implements aggressive regulations.

Such control undermines individual initiative because equal distribution of wealth discourages effort.

When workers and non-workers get the same income, the incentive to work goes downhill.

People are prevented from enjoying the fruits of their labor.

The action-outcome principle being violated, production suffers, as does agency.

The earth has sufficient resources to take care of billions of God's children and stock their fridges with leftovers to boot.

> For the earth is full, and there is enough and to spare; yea, I prepared all things, and have given unto the children of men to be agents unto themselves.[9]

Okay, call us the fat earth society.

But it takes work to turn raw materials into finished products. The pie expands and contracts according to man's efforts. **It is not a finite, self-existing pie as socialism assumes.**

Socialists want everyone to have a basic income (a guaranteed freedom from failure) and seek to punish the rich in the name of social justice for taking too much of the supposed finite pie. But having a greater <u>share</u> is not the same as having a greater <u>amount</u>. In fact, the amount will always be less than in a free-market economy, illusory percentage share notwithstanding.

> If one looks only at percentages, 70% of X appears a much better deal than 10% of Y. But what if X=$10 and Y=$1000?

When people know their earnings are destined for redistribution, they will produce less of it and society's wealth will shrink. To keep up the farcical face of fairness, a socialist government will inevitably borrow money. Which leads to debt to be repaid … when?

Redistributing today's wealth is bad enough. **Redistributing the wealth that is yet to be earned is exponentially worse.** In the first case, government is acting upon people who are already living; in the second, it is acting on the unborn – those who will have to pay off the debt incurred before they were born. Or upon whom hyperinflation will fall.

Such debt accumulation for socialistic payouts is pure and simple acting upon others – pulling the strings that turn people into objects.

That equal possession of resources can never be accomplished is immaterial to its leading advocates. **The mere attempt provides them power.** Wherever full socialism has been tried, leaders lived in luxury while their subjects suffered, even starved.

The conveniently named "vanguard of the proletariat" – the Politburo – in the Soviet Union lived lavishly as they worked "to suffuse workers with socialist consciousness."[10] Venezuela's Hugo Chavez became a billionaire in American dollars (his daughter still is) while the bolivars pictured above became worthless. While his people shivered in the dark, Nicolae Ceausescu of Romania commanded that fireplaces in his numerous homes be kept burning so they would be warm should he drop in. Those who agitate for socialism the most are those least likely to tolerate being one of the masses.

Let these observations tickle your dendrites:

> "The democracy will cease to exist when you take away from those who are willing to work and give to those who would not." – Thomas Jefferson

> "A claim for equality of material position can be met only by a government with totalitarian power." – F.A. Hayek

> "The urge to save humanity is almost always only a false-face for the urge to rule it." – H.L. Mencken

> "The problem with socialism is that you eventually run out of other people's money." – Margaret Thatcher

By misappropriating the fruits of one's labor, socialism violates a central feature of agency – that we are put on earth to act, to do, to accomplish. In so doing, socialism is the enemy of creativity, innovation, refinement, prosperity, and progress.

"Throughout history under its various regimes, in its pursuit of a spurious utopia equality," argues Joseph Epstein, "socialism has produced no great art, profound thinkers or enduring science. It has been death on entrepreneurship."[11]

III. The Promise of Equal Outcomes Weakens Responsibility

Most people want equality of opportunity.
Socialists want equality of outcome.

Equal effort from everyone is impossible.

No units of effort → one unit of reward = injustice
One unit of effort → one unit of reward = justice
Two units of effort → one unit of reward = injustice

When efforts are proportionally rewarded,
there is justice and incentive to work and progress.

When rewards are disproportionate to effort, however,
there is no incentive to work, no progress, and no justice.

Equal opportunity expands agency.
Equal outcome destroys justice.

If there is no justice, God ceases to be God.[12]

Once people believe in socialism and that government will wield the power of wealth equitably, they must necessarily believe equality of outcomes is possible and fair. And further the implausible extension that everyone can be put on a level playing field and kept there. Without force, they naïvely believe.

No two people are alike. We are all on a ladder of **natural inequality**.

These two facts do exist, that there are two spirits, one being more intelligent than the other; there shall be another more intelligent than they; I am the Lord thy God, I am more intelligent than they all.[13]

And …

Whatever principle of intelligence we attain unto in this life, it will rise with us in the resurrection. And if a person gains more knowledge and intelligence in this life through his diligence and obedience than another, he will have so much the advantage in the world to come.[14]

Because **people differ**, especially in effort, their **achievements will always be unequal**. Socialism's vaunted equal distribution of wealth is unsustainable and can never produce the equality of mankind they brag about.

It's simple. Let's say a socialist government gives everyone $5000 a month for a year. The equality wouldn't last 30 days because people would spend it differently. Some will spend wisely, others will squander. Some will save, lend and/or invest. After not many $5K distributions, people will notice others better off and will clamor to make everyone "equal" again.

> Building socialism that works is like building a snowman in the Sahara.

There are three kingdoms in heaven. Not just one.

Similarly, Brigham Young observed that those who "would divide the substance of the rich among the poor, and make all what they call equal" would cause him to question "how long would it be before a certain portion of them would be calling upon the other portion for something with which to sustain themselves?"[15]

Wealth redistribution to bring about lasting equality is impossible.

And socialist leaders won't care. They enjoy power while true believers search for the holy grail, the true socialism that has yet to be tried.

Consider how this impacts responsibility. As socialism redistributes a society's ever-decreasing wealth, more people will **excuse themselves from helping others** – the "I only have enough for me" thinking.

What do we do with the fruits of our labor? Do we willingly feed the hungry? Clothe the naked? Care for the sick? Agonizing questions when one has a diminishing paycheck.

"The state is the great fictitious entity by which everyone seeks to live at the expense of everyone else."

– Frederic Bastiat

But now add the soothing song of socialism: "Don't worry; we will establish a classless society where there are no rich and no poor, where everyone is equal." The human nature response? "Oh, what a relief. I don't have to worry about others. The state will take care of them."

Look up accountable and responsible and the connecting principle is stewardship – what we do with the resources the Lord blesses us with by having us work for them. But if we work and the state takes the fruits of our labor, there is **no personal stewardship**. And one of God's purposes for our earthly existence is ignored.

Socialism thus defeats stewardship, robs us of chances to progress by reducing a sense of responsibility, and hinders agency.

And it does so **under the guise of helping others**, counterfeit as can be. (As Thoreau wrote, "If I knew for a certainty that a man was coming to my house with the conscious design of doing me good, I should run for my life.") If we allow socialism, we are allowing the state to take care of others and may be reminded of Scrooge who, when asked for a donation to help the poor, fobbed off personal responsibility and replied, "Are there no prisons ... workhouses?"[16]

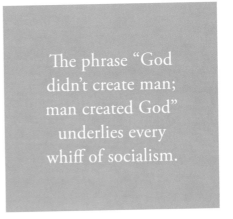

The phrase "God didn't create man; man created God" underlies every whiff of socialism.

Now, some may contend that unequal efforts in keeping the commandments must necessarily lead to something less than living with God for eternity. The difference here is the grace of Christ. We cannot merit exaltation by ourselves; unequal efforts will cause us to fall short. And not everyone in the celestial kingdom will have put in the same efforts. There's no way the average celestial kingdom dweller can equal the effort and deeds of an Abraham, Moses, Peter, or Joseph Smith. But if the effort is sufficient and the intentions of the heart are sufficient, the **grace and mercy of Christ** will make up the shortfall.

Satan has no such power to make up anybody's shortfall whatever their goals. Nor would he ever help people if he did. That is why he constantly works for equality of outcomes, by force if necessary.

And such "equality" if ever gained will be a bland and boring sameness – everyone equally poor.

No one has ever climbed over barbed wire to flee a free-market capitalism nation and enter a socialism country.

IV. Forced Philanthropy Robs Fruits of Labor

In 1944, President Franklin Roosevelt called for passage into law a Second Bill of Rights, aka an Economic Bill of Rights. Among these were the right to food, housing, jobs, education, and health care, government being the designated enforcer. The effort was defeated, but today's socialists are resurrecting the idea.

To remedy the inequality they bemoan, socialists would grant everyone automatic rights to society's resources, no matter the origin of that wealth.

They believe the basics of life should be free.

Man-made rights are mandates people can demand at the expense of others.

The natural God-given rights of life, liberty and the pursuit of happiness, on the other hand, do not cost others anything.

Mandated rights in contrast create forced philanthropy.

They harm the productive by taking away motivation and the right to choose how to use the fruits of one's labor.

Such will also harm recipients because many will reduce efforts and thus violate God's commandment to act, do, and accomplish.

Four points to ponder.

First, with my thanks to philosophy professor Brian Thomassen, note the blessing and uniqueness of the Declaration of Independence's model of life, liberty, and pursuit of happiness. As inspired by Locke and others, it allows liberty to develop and thrive. Using freedom of speech or owning private property (fruits of one's labor being essential to such happiness) as examples, one is neither required to speak out or buy land, but the *capacity* is there. This necessarily disempowers the state.

> With socialism, people wait for bread. With capitalism, bread waits for people.

By comparison, the first-blush, similar-sounding French model of liberty, equality, and fraternity, as inspired by Rousseau, provides no clear way for citizens to be equal or have a natural fraternity – some are richer or more powerful, while others are more self-interested and/or less empathetic toward others. Under this tradition, to provide for collective equality or brotherliness, something must have the power to impose such notions on the citizenry. Hello, coercive government.

Second, under the above socialism idea, we must **involuntarily** give up a portion of the fruits of our labor. Under Christian ideals, we should **voluntarily** share. In which case are the fruits most likely to be squandered or subverted for personal gain?

Does my Christian obligation to feed the hungry constitute a hungry person's right to take what I have? Have I fulfilled my gospel obligation to feed the hungry if I vote for someone who promises to raise taxes to that end? Will such count as good works?

While socialism says *must*, Christianity says *should.* And failing to do so? Under socialism, punishment. With Christianity, absence of reward. Which is the better long-run motivator?

> You have the right
> to pursue happiness.
> Others are not
> obligated to provide it.

Third, where will the list of man-made rights end? For example, does one have a right to a good life? If so, a good life depends on having a healthy heart. Using the same logic as the Second Bill of Rights, everyone has the right to a healthy heart, which in turn means someone with a failing heart has the right to a heart transplant. But what if there are more people desiring a heart than there are donors? The list of man-made rights – "you get to be the donor" – quickly becomes absurd.

Fourth, if a society establishes rights, that society as then constituted should bear the costs – feel the consequences. Here again the problem of a third-party opportunistic buttinsky. Where there is a third-party intrusion (whether it be another person, a government, or the adversary), agency is damaged. **The free market as a two-party transaction is natural; socialism as a three-party arrangement is not. Whenever the state is the intermediary between giver and receiver, mischief results**:

- The state will take just enough from the productive so they won't rebel, and it will go into debt for the rest of what was promised the receiver.

- Consequences are delayed and the next generation has to pick up the bill.

- Politicians will use such delays of consequence to buy votes and grab power.

- Bureaucrats will siphon off a generous "handling" charge.

If a benefit is immediate and the cost deferred, people do not feel pain and the benefit is perceived as free, precisely what socialists want because they will take credit for helping the poor. Somebody in the future will have to pay the bill for those new rights, but that doesn't seem to concern those who benefit.

We have a tremendous national debt because of **consequence shifting**. Stretching out the day of reckoning will in time interfere with the action-consequence principle, and therefore violate agency.

The day will come when a new generation will say, "Why should we pay for a hospital bill incurred in 2020?" "Why should we pay for a meal somebody in Toledo ate before we were even born?"

V. Socialism Strangles Motivation – A Classroom Experiment

Capitalism is based on 3 Ps:
prices, profit-and-loss, private property rights.

Each of these is an incentive-enhancing component.

Socialism fails because it is inconsistent with
fundamental principles of human behavior.

It is a system that <u>ignores incentives</u>.

Socialism assumes we know all we need
to know so things can be managed.

It assumes that people will work as hard
for others as they do for themselves.

Further, it assumes motivation is a constant;
the size of the reward for work is immaterial.

A greater blindness to human nature is hard to imagine.

Every few years, a story about socialism pops up on the Internet that substitutes equality of college grades for equal distribution of wealth. This apocryphal but useful parable provides a better angle of clarity than when people think only in dollars:

> Students in a college economics class argued that socialism worked and that no one would be poor and no one would be rich, a great equalizer.
>
> The professor said, "OK, let's experiment. All grades will be averaged and everyone will receive the same grade."
>
> After the first test, the grades were averaged and everyone got a B. The students who studied hard were upset and the students who studied little were happy. As the second test rolled around, the students who studied little had studied even less and the ones who studied hard decided they too wanted a free ride, so they studied little.
>
> The second test average was a D. No one was happy.
>
> When students took the third test, everyone received an F.
>
> Over the course of the tests, scores never increased as bickering, blame and name-calling led to hard feelings. No one would study for the benefit of anyone else.
>
> Every student failed the class but learned a great lesson – that socialism, whether applied to the economy or college grades, will always fail. When the reward is great, the effort to succeed is great, but when government takes all the reward away, no one will try or want to succeed.
>
> So predictable. They achieved the hyped goal of socialism, but the equality was boring, miserable, and resented. Socialism stamps out the variety that makes life enjoyable.

❧

This lesson has been learned the hard way in our own land.

Pilgrims in the famous Plymouth Colony, America's first socialist republic, tried cultivating crops in common for two years. They nearly starved to death. Governor William Bradford recorded that …

"… the less industrious members of the colony came late to their work in the fields, and were slow and easy in their labors. Knowing that they and their families were to receive an equal share of whatever the group produced, they saw little reason to be more diligent in their efforts. The harder working among the colonists became resentful that their efforts would be redistributed to the more malingering members of the colony. Soon they, too, were coming late to work and were less energetic in the fields."[17]

> "Socialism in general has a record of failure so blatant that only an intellectual could ignore or evade it."
>
> – Thomas Sowell

So they abandoned the idea of communal property and gave each his own land. Guess what? Governor Bradford again: "It made all hands very industrious … and much more corn was planted than otherwise would have been."

Same experience in the colony of Jamestown, Virginia. Of 104 men in 1607, only 38 survived the first year of communal living. After the experiment was abandoned, Captain John Smith observed, "When our people were fed out of the common store, and labored jointly together, glad was he who could slip from his labor or slumber over his task …. We reaped not so much corn from the labors of thirty, as now three or four do provide for themselves."[18]

Both experiences demonstrate that socialism is based on faulty principles inconsistent with human behavior. When these early inhabitants of our country finally woke to reality, **they established property rights and free-market enterprise and prospered**.

Sadly, some today don't learn from history. Panera Cares, a socialism experiment of its parent Panera Bread, had to close its doors. Customers were asked to pay what they felt they could afford or felt like. It was mobbed by students and the homeless. Students ate without paying and the homeless would eat every meal there, paying very little. All told, the restaurant covered less than 70% of its total costs.[19]

The same thing happened with Israel's communal kibbutzim. Voluntary socialism? Back to the drawing boards.

Five morals from such stories:[20]

1. You cannot legislate the poor into prosperity by legislating the wealthy out of prosperity.

2. What one person receives without working for, another person must work for without receiving.

3. The government cannot give to anybody anything that the government does not first take from somebody else.

4. You cannot multiply wealth by dividing it!

5. When half of the people get the idea that they do not have to work because the other half is going to take care of them, and when the other half gets the idea that it does no good to work because somebody else is going to get what they work for, that is the beginning of the end of any nation.

Socialists think they can change one part of a system and the other parts will keep going as if nothing had happened – that they can dump a boulder into one end of a pond and not cause ripples at the other.

VI. Lack of Capital Undermines Creativity – Curiosity Withers

Under socialism's tut-tuts, pursuing gain is greed. To socialists, money is but an evil medium for the exchange of goods; people should own no more than immediate needs require. They fail to see how pooling it stimulates creativity.

Creativity is powered by dreams of success.

Success in turn depends on freedom of action and investment capital to flourish those dreams.

Socialism's tight controls are anathema to freedom and make it difficult to create new capital for investments.

Available capital also dwindles as certain citizens pressure government for higher taxes on the rich.

Excitement about engineering an idea into existence fades if investment capital is sparse, socialistic controls plentiful, and potential rewards few.

As hopes for success fade, the mind loses curiosity and entertains fewer connections.

Socialism thus stifles creativity, a great fruit of agency.

Imagine for a moment you're an entrepreneur. You have a creative idea for a new product, but you know you must risk money and effort:

If the combined risk of money and effort equals a dollar, would you risk it for a potential reward of $100? Of course.

If the cost of the risk is $99, would you do it for $100? Of course not.

You have to decide your risk-and-comfort level before you act.

Now let's say government announces a 20% tax on your product. Your potential reward is now $80, your comfort level changes, and what you're willing to risk proportionally decreases.

Even worse, let's say a new law limits your return on investment – that a large profit (however defined) isn't fair in a society where people should be equal. Under a profit ceiling, how much would you risk? Would you proceed with your idea if your dollar-and-effort investment of $100 would merely afford you the chance to sell your product for only a possible, but not guaranteed, $110 payday?

You see where this is going. It doesn't take onerous wealth taxes before the risks become too great proportionate to the rewards to justify further involvement. The potential reward doesn't have to be zero to kill motivation.

And rewards quickly become small under socialism because those in charge can change the rules whenever and how much they want. The reward-to-risk ratio thus out of whack, especially for long-term investments, creativity dies and money for investment in other ideas will never be accumulated.

The drive for equality of outcome sooner or later kills agency and all the progress that could have happened.

Ludwig von Mises observed:

"Socialism is not in the least what it pretends to be. It is not the pioneer of a better and finer world, but the spoiler of what thousands of years of civilization have created. **It does not build; it destroys**. For destruction is the essence of it. It produces nothing, it only consumes what the social order based on private ownership of the means of production has created."[21]

So what does private ownership create that socialism does not?

First, a **willingness to save, pool, and invest** money. Because socialism is a monopoly, advocates give little thought that capital is needed to form new ventures and conduct the research and development needed before new products generate profits, which in turn drive prosperity. People shy from creating investment capital if the state controls prices and profits.

Second, **productivity**. As people under socialism have less money to spend and invest, fewer will be the opportunities to risk, act, and produce something. And correspondingly less willingness to act as people realize they will be paid the same whether they work hard or not, whether they put their capital to work or not.

Money is also more likely to be spent for short-term needs and less likely to be invested for long-term returns if wages and prices are controlled.

Third, **creative thinking**. When we know investment capital from a free-market system is available for promising products, our neurons and dendrites kick in, our imagination expands, and we get excited our own ideas might hit pay dirt.

Fourth, **an entrepreneurial spirit**. Posing as humanitarians, socialists believe those who earn money beyond daily needs are greedy. Hardly encouragement for citizens to go the extra mile. The profit motive is integral to the creative spirit; enterprise ceases when a system restricts us to our daily bread.

You can vote your
way into socialism,
but you have to
shoot your way out.

In all four of these situations, socialism diminishes agency because it kills the human spirit, discourages creativity, distorts investment, and fails to reward productive risk.

President Ezra Taft Benson said: "Yes, we have traveled a long way down the soul-destroying road of socialism …. How did it happen? Men of expediency ascended to high political offices by **promising what was not theirs to give**, and citizens voted them into office in the hopes of **receiving what they had not earned**."[22]

VII. Socialism Violates Choice – Eliminates Competition

Jay Gould, one of the most unscrupulous men in American history, held a monopoly on transatlantic telegraphy in the 1880's, and having no competition gouged his customers. He met his come-uppance when John Mackay, a big believer in free enterprise and the miner who hit the Big Bonanza in Nevada silver, laid a competing transatlantic cable that broke Gould's stranglehold and brought down prices.[23]

In contrast, socialists view competition as evil because it runs counter to their vision of a communal cooperative society – a utopia of all working together for the common good. Their operating dictum is, to quote Marx, "From each according to his ability, to each according to his needs." (It should be "…to each according to his *deeds*.")

Competition makes such "take-and-give" practices, let alone calculations, nearly impossible and therefore must be controlled, preferably eliminated, they reason.

<u>Businesses</u> prefer to be monopolies,
but they know their competitors prefer the same.

So they work harder to win customers –
produce a better product for a lower price.

Entrepreneurs become more innovative
and customers get more choices.

Robust competition prevents monopolies.

<u>Power-seekers</u> also prefer to be a monopoly.

They fear, really fear, other power-seekers.

So they go one better – rather than a better product for
a lower price, they promise a something for a nothing.

When apologists say the "right" socialism hasn't yet
been tried, they really mean true socialists
haven't had sufficient power.

The socialism they envision is a monopoly on <u>all</u> power,
political and economic – Deep State on steroids.

Therefore, competition in the marketplace
is a natural enemy to socialism because it hinders
control of the production and distribution of wealth.

Competition drives progress.
Kill competition and you kill progress.

Socialists want to eliminate competition and the messy friction of the marketplace. They want people to be equal – eventually communal – in all things and speak passionately about equality, peace, harmony, belonging, togetherness, and the common good of mankind. All desirable goals and we will yet have them, but to usher them in by force is not God's plan for our progress.

God's plan for our use of His gift of **agency centers on the key verb to act**. We carefully weigh our options, make our best decision, accept the risk, and then it's "Tally ho the fox."

> # If competition were eliminated, what would be the fun of sports?

The *friction* of competition and the *risks* of action are thus intertwined.

Advocates of socialism seem not to realize these two things are critical to productivity. Friction and risk cannot be eliminated in a healthy society any more than we can eliminate the necessary "opposition in all things." Too many who fight for access to the marketplace when they begin their careers are, unfortunately, only too willing to plead for protections from friction and risk when they have succeeded. "I'm in; shut the door; protect me from competition."

Known as crony capitalists, such people want favoritism and privileges – an economy in which …

> "… businesses thrive not as a result of risk taken by them, but rather, as a return on money amassed through a **nexus between a business class and the political class**. This is done using state power to crush genuine competition in handing out permits, government grants, special tax breaks, or other forms of state intervention. … Entrepreneurship and innovative practices, which seek to reward risk, are stifled …."[24]

Socialists see such monopolists as evidence of capitalism's rot. (In a Q&A session in Russia, one person attending our lectures actually asked, "In the West is it acceptable to 'burn out' a competitor?") But there's nothing free-market about using government connections to eliminate competition and avoid risk. In reality, **both crony capitalists and socialists favor monopoly**; it's merely a matter of who gets to do the monopolizing.

Those who believe competition is a trait of ultimate socialism point to the Stakhanovite movement in the Soviet Union. Yes, it was a form of competition in which people competed, but **the goal was recognition** (Order of Lenin, Hero of Socialist Labor, etc.) by outworking others, **not the competition that leads to innovation** and improved ways of doing things. This showcase contest was controlled by the state for state purposes – who can mine the most coal for the benefit of the state? – not the competition that improves one's personal life through free-market mechanisms and better rewards for mankind in general. Stakhanovite production mainly improved the power and comfort of autocratic leaders.[25]

Destroying free-will competition is the avowed goal of socialism. Because they share this same goal, crony capitalists are but shadow socialists in disguise.

The Invincible Free Market

Socialism causes problems; the free market solves them.

As the Soviet Union was crumbling, I was part of a delegation invited to Russia to explain how a multi-party system works. We were guests of the government and given lodging in the best hotel in each city. Checking in at one hotel, I noticed a big box, easily two feet high, of golden raisins sitting next to the manager's desk. Quite out of place. So I asked our Russian host why.

"You must understand," he explained, "for years people have been told they belong to the glorious communist society where the people have everything in common. They therefore reason, 'Well, if everything belongs to the people, I'll just take this [such as the box of raisins] as my share.'" And it doesn't occur to them that they're stealing.

So what does the hotel manager do with the raisins? "She lets friends know what she has and asks what they would like to trade for them." Barter.

Got that? The moment subjects of socialism have something they feel is theirs, they turn to a free-market mechanism to improve their lot in life!

A member of our delegation, Bruce Hughes, talked with a dentist who attended our lectures and learned that state control of health care caused a six-month waiting period before a patient could be seen. "But what if I have a severe tooth ache?" he asked. The dentist matter-of-factly replied, "You either buy someone else's appointment or bring two chickens to my house on the weekend."

The free market again. That the dentist assumed an appointment slot would be for sale suggests underground capitalism already at work. If it doesn't cost anything to make a dentist appointment, entrepreneurs have a free commodity that becomes of value as the date approaches. *Talk about buying low and selling high!*

Historian Lee Edwards summarizes the promises and contradictory realities of socialism:[26]

- Socialists promise a classless society but create the prison camps of the Gulag.

- They assure peace but engage in wars of national liberation.

- They abolish private property but depend upon the underground economy.

- They stamp out religion but worship Big Brother.
- They bring down corrupt dictators but institute a dictatorship of the Party.
- Socialism is a pseudo-religion founded in pseudo-science and enforced by political tyranny.

To sum it up: Under socialism, politics and power set society's course. Under agency, freedom and creativity and power to act set the individual's course. **Agency is person centered; socialism is state centered.**

Or to put a lighter touch on it, socialism turns the economy into a giant Department of Motor Vehicles.

❧

"Socialism of any type and shade leads to a total destruction of the human spirit and to a leveling of mankind into death."
– Alexander Solzhenitsyn

Chapter 19

Tyranny
Surveillance, Fear, Control

"The accumulation of all powers, legislative, executive, and judiciary, in the same hands, whether of one, a few, or many, and whether hereditary, self-appointed, or elective, may justly be pronounced the very definition of tyranny."

– James Madison

Communism is the goal of socialism's relentless advocates. Though today's tyrants are just as power-hungry as Stalin, Hitler, and Mao, technology has given them greater control over their unfortunate subjects without the need for as much mass violence.

The tyranny of total control began
with pride and the wisdom of the world –
the great and abominable church in the
large and spacious building.

Then came numerous rules that intimidate
followed by vague rules that cause
uncertainty and fear.

Tyrannies of the past maintained control
by large scale visible violence.

Today's tyrannies employ violence when needed,
but total control arises from thorough
surveillance abetted by technology.

Totalitarian governments use rewards as well as
punishments to yield desired conformity.

As fear of making a mistake goes up,
willingness to choose and act goes down.

As willingness to act goes down,
people are more subject to being acted upon.

As surveillance, fear, and intimidation increase,
freedom goes down, control goes up,
and agency is lost.

When my previously mentioned delegation went to the Soviet Union to explain how political campaigning in a multi-party system works, the topic one afternoon was coalition building. We talked strategy and tactics and then divided them into teams with instructions to brainstorm which groups they would go after to build a coalition of voters sufficient for victory. After 45 minutes, we reassembled and asked the first team to give their report.

The team leader said, "The first people we want on our side are the waiters." Waiters? Hearing the answer through the translator, I thought I'd misunderstood so I let the conversation continue. Then came the second team and the leader said, "We also want the waiters first."

I called time out and asked how many teams had waiters as their top group in their coalition-building efforts. *All the hands went up.* I asked why and the looks on their faces told me I was naïve about how things worked in the good old USSR. One team leader explained, "Well, everybody knows that all the waiters are KGB and they listen in on all the conversations. **They know everything about everybody and we want them on our side.**"

❧

China – New-Tech Tyranny

The People's Republic of China doesn't need snoopy waiters overhearing gossip. Leaders use technology and have positioned over 200 *million* surveillance cameras to record what people do, a figure scheduled to triple within the next few years. One camera for every seven people!

When Big Brother has 200,000,000 eyeballs, soon to increase to 600,000,000, little escapes notice.

President Xi Jinping's minions use advanced facial recognition technology and analysis of internet activity to **control society through social credit points**. If you pay your bills on time, follow traffic rules, and participate in activities deemed friendly to the state, you build up a high score and get such perks as visas, access to higher-class products, and opportunities to send your kids to better schools. If, on the other hand, you spend too much on alcohol, too much time playing videogames, don't stop at crosswalks, complain about the government, or "disturb the public order," you'll get a low social credit score and find you "cannot easily eat in restaurants, register at hotels, purchase products, or travel freely."[1] Each citizen is digitized.

> Beijing the capital was once Anglicized as Peking. Too bad they changed it – a Peking order would fit perfectly.

It is so pervasive that if you steal a bicycle, the police will be there to greet you when you ride it home … and deduct points, to say the least. An article in the *South China Morning Post* elaborates that police now use special glasses with facial-recognition software to quickly scan faces and immediately be notified whether a person is wanted.[2]

China even has scanners on recycling bins and trucks. Thousands of pictures of garbage are analyzed using artificial intelligence techniques to determine whether people are correctly recycling waste. If they do, they get points; if not, a visit from a neighborhood committee[3] – the use by tyrants of low-self-esteem people to keep an eye on others. So the obvious observation: if they care that much about garbage, what won't they try to observe about people?

Certain actions trigger the harshest of penalties. China executes more people than any other nation, which might be expected given its population, but the number of crimes punishable by death is 46, the highest in the world. Even possessing relatively small amounts of drugs (as low as 10 grams in some cases) can be punished by lethal injection or firing squad.[4] Executions often occur in modified 24-seat vans, the government claiming they are more humane and cost less than firing squads.[5]

That people are aware of 40-some execution vans rolling around the country can't be without impact. Add to it the usual tyrannies of gulags and the current "re-education" camps visited upon Uighur minorities in Xinjiang province, and the combination keeps Chinese society in line.

More details how Beijing handles the Muslim Uighur community have come to light via a leaked memo from the region's top security official instructing those who run the re-education camps to treat people as if in a high security prison. As reported by BBC News, the government memo includes orders to never allow escapes and to ensure full video surveillance free of blind spots. Camp supervisors are further instructed to "implement behavioural norms and discipline requirements for getting up, roll call, washing, going to the toilet, organizing and housekeeping, eating, studying, sleeping, closing the door and so forth."[6]

When a government disciplines use of toilets, doors and beds, and especially the "so forth," it's difficult to imagine any activity left to man's agency.

The threat of such concentration camps will always be an ever-ready tool in a high-tech tyranny's arsenal.

> "When the people fear their government, there is tyranny; when the government fears the people, there is liberty."
>
> – Thomas Jefferson

Watch What You Say

Visitors to China on business tell of conversation boundary lines. Discourse between business people is free and easy as long as the topic remains business. But ask a question about social policies, worldviews, or Hong Kong, smiles fade, conversation stiffens, and some even leave the room. And especially don't ask about the three T's: Taiwan, Tibet, and Tiananmen Square.

The average citizen's knowledge about China's recent history, let alone the rest of the world, is limited. A traveler told me about a bus ride to the Great Wall on which the tour guide spoke about Chinese history up to the mid-20th century. When she got to Mao, she told of the good things he did and then said, "Mao made some mistakes. *We don't know what those mistakes were because we don't learn them in school.* But we know he made mistakes and the new leaders corrected them." Nothing to see here; move along.

When visitors to China step into a taxi or the country's version of Ubers, they'd be wise to assume the buggy is bugged. It is especially the case for the few foreigners granted permission to visit Tibet, as the state does not want them to have free contact with Tibetans who, in solid numbers, support the real Dalai Lama, not the Chinese substitute.

Russia requires the Tinder dating app to store six months of data and to hand it over to the FSB intelligence agency on demand.[7]

In fact, all conversations throughout China are of interest to its leaders, and all visitors are advised to act as if they're speaking into a microphone, which indeed they are. Those who want a private conversation will either take a walk where street noise muffles their talk or go to a noisy restaurant. They assume that all conversations in public places are recorded.

Corporate Conformity

High-tech tyranny continues as the undergirding social credit system is now applied to businesses to punish or reward companies based on corporate behavior. Not only local businesses, but especially the international business community. The system collects information whether a company is following China's draconian rules and regulations and uses the results to calculate a social-credit score from which administrators decide whether a corporation is allowed to purchase land, establish markets, and otherwise participate in the Chinese economy.[8]

All of this on top of well-known stories about China's centralized planning applied to the average citizen – you will study this subject and then be sent to city X to work. **Little if any opportunity for the non-elite on their own volition to choose, act, experience, and learn – to exercise agency**.

Some point to China as a good example of proper socialism, and it may well be from the perspective of those who rule, but this hi-tech communism is hardly the "it's free" utopia the less perceptive think is coming. The state may not presently own the means of production or specify wages and prices, but there is no doubt they determine who may.

A single goal summarizes Communism: **the abolition of private property**. When one cannot own the fruits of one's labor, prosperity and agency wither.

A recent report states that Mr. Xi, who *believes China is the world's only legitimate state*, "is recombining already large state enterprises back into formal monopolies and duopolies, reversing the partial privatization of earlier years, having the state buy shares in listed private companies, shoveling more state subsidies to favored state businesses, exercising tighter control over price movements in equity markets…" and so on.[9]

While it has incorporated enough free-market principles to produce modernity in the cities, the system with its heavy doses of favoritism exists for one reason: **to advance government control**. Others share in the goodies only as they conform to the wishes of party leaders.

The story is told of a company that started an innovative business of allowing people to rent bicycles using their phones, ride them wherever they wanted, and just leave them there for the next person. Their success attracted competition. One day the original company ran an ad during a holiday event that local communist officials found objectionable. Within three months the company was out of business and a competitor more submissive to party whims took over the market.

Free-market shirts and pants; socialism underwear.

> "The position of this Church on the subject of Communism has never changed. We consider it the greatest satanical threat to peace, prosperity, and the spread of God's work among men that exists on the face of the earth."[10]
>
> – David O. McKay

To protect their power, China's leaders attribute economic progress to patriotism rather than the free market. The best of both worlds as they suppose: massive surveillance data systems (aided in no small measure by American technology and inventions[11]), extensive control, people in limited-behavior boxes, state-subservient entrepreneurship, clean cities, obedient minds, and the trains run on time.

Agency for the average citizen? Miniscule.

Amalickiah – The Path to the Top

A prime example of how someone becomes all powerful is explained in the 46th chapter of Alma. The key is to capitalize on dissent:

And Amalickiah was desirous to be a king; and those people who were **wroth** were also desirous that he should be their king; and they were the greater part of them the lower judges of the land, and **they were seeking for power**.

They were already part of government but wanted more power. So the formula is find those who already have partial power and **flatter** them – "you deserve better" – and promise them more, as we have discussed. It's the pattern of almost all tyrants.

And they had been led by the flatteries of Amalickiah, that if they would support him and establish him to be their king that **he would make them rulers over the people**.

And there were many in the church who believed in the flattering words of Amalickiah, therefore they dissented even from the church; and thus were the affairs of the people of Nephi exceedingly precarious and dangerous ....

Yea, we see that Amalickiah, because he was a man of **cunning device** and a man of **many flattering words**, that he led away the hearts of many people to do wickedly; yea, and to seek to destroy the church of God, and to destroy the foundation of liberty which God had granted unto them ....

And Gadianton himself also followed the formula.

Therefore he did flatter them ... that if they would place him in the judgment-seat he would [place them] in **power and authority** among the people ....[12]

Part of the flattery process is securing the loyalty of those who themselves thirst for power. Riches for servile toadies who execute the wishes of the top tyrant are part of the formula, and at times even a goodly dose of prosperity for the lower-ranked obedient sweeten the incentives and preserve his power.

Ask a communist how he visualizes himself in a future communist society. He will not see himself as a worker, but as a party official telling others what to do.

Those Who Dig the Pit …

Tyranny doesn't have to be bloody for despots to control a society, but occasional "incidents" can prove helpful to the dictator. The final step in tyranny is when the leader gets rid of his lieutenants who helped him get to the top of the heap. It signals the masses, "Don't get any ideas."

David Bronstein traveled to Mexico in the 1930s and settled down to his passion of writing. Oh, he'd had some dealings that had gone sour and had to know that former colleagues were after him to settle a few debts. In fact, he even wrote a book detailing his side of the story and how he interpreted events.[13] But one summer day in 1940 as he was sitting in his study, an assassin snuck up on him and planted an icepick in his brain.

Evil never forgets one of its own. You see, David Bronstein was born Lev Davidovich Bronstein, later known as … Leon Trotsky, exiled Soviet Politburo member and Joseph Stalin's chief rival.

History lists numerous other examples of people who dug a pit for others and ended up in it themselves:

> Fearing the growing power of Ernst Röhm, leader of the Storm Troopers or Brownshirts, Hitler had him and dozens of additional competitors for power shot in a 72-hour period known as the Night of the Long Knives.[14]

In what became known as the Great Purge, paranoid Stalin accused hundreds of thousands of fellow communists of espionage and conspiracies and had them executed or sent to labor camps. Many of the secret police who carried out the purge were themselves later executed.[15]

Mao Zedong feared the popularity of Liu Shaoqi, third most powerful leader in China for 15 years. Liu was purged for disagreeing with Mao and died under harsh treatment.[16]

Kim Jong Un of North Korea executed his own uncle and scores of other relatives and acquaintances in positions of power.[17]

We know that "it is by the wicked that the wicked are punished,"[18] but where power is craved, cut-throat competition is more than a phrase. When you hear of a dictator turning on his colleagues, you can be sure tyranny is becoming more entrenched.

What's In The Works?

When Alma was kicked out of Ammonihah, an angel of the Lord told him to return:

> For behold, they do _study_ at this time that they may destroy the liberty of thy people ....[19]

Hmm. What did such people study? Philosophy, law, politics ...? We don't know except it had to be a body of knowledge. Perhaps a syllabus assigned for Secret Combinations 404 ("they are had among all people"[20]), Gadianton robbers being the professors. At any rate, it undoubtedly had to do with pride and elitism and power – looking down on people who believed in such archaic concepts as liberty. We're told further in that verse that their activity "is contrary to the statutes, and judgments, and commandments which [the Lord] has given unto his people."

Why wouldn't this pattern be a warning for our day – that there are people who systematically study how to overthrow liberty?

Another Book of Mormon prophecy describes this same process that begins with pride and ends with hell:

> And [a] great pit, which hath been digged for them by that great and abominable church, ... was founded by the devil ... that he might lead away the souls of men down to hell – yea, that great pit which hath been digged for the destruction of men shall be filled by those who digged it, unto their utter destruction ... according to the captivity of the devil, and also according to the justice of God ....[21]

Note the components:

The great pit founded by devil: obviously hell, Satan's kingdom.

The great and abominable church: the wisdom of the world, the pride that begins the first of gradually sneaky steps of people being acted upon.

That he might lead away the souls of men down to hell: the path from being an agent to becoming an object.

Those who digged it: Satan's converts who create the earthly mechanisms that diminish and destroy agency, to which such -isms they, themselves, also fall prey. (Gives new meaning to a once-cool phrase.)

Utter destruction: the total loss of agency.

According to the justice of God: he who destroys agency is consigned to the captivity of the devil.

The hell which hath no end: stagnation, no progress, no agency.

What concerns me about the future is not only the obvious threat from China, but that quasi-socialist, wannabe dictators in other countries will follow the China model. They're the type who will give favored groups enough freedom to produce bountifully, take a goodly share for themselves, but still control the population through surveillance, social credits, intimidation, and fear.

So as tech-oriented tyranny spreads, as ideologues weigh in with their perspectives, and commentators offer their slant, how should we as regular citizens decide where to stand on the issues of our day to protect our agency? May I suggest we ask ourselves seven simple questions:

- How free am I to act on my thoughts and choices?

- Are consequences proportionate to actions?

- Are society's rules reasonable or oppressive?

- Are leaders subject to the same rules?

- Am I being unreasonably observed or monitored?

- Am I my own agent or is someone else pulling the strings?

- And especially ... **which of the available policy options will best strengthen the agency of each individual citizen?**

&

A fitting reminder from Elder David A. Bednar:

"You and I are not objects. We are agents. We are blessed with agency because of the atonement of Christ. And with that agency, we are to act and not be acted upon. That agency gives us the capacity to determine how we will respond to the variety of challenges we will experience in the flesh."[22]

Progress

Chapter 20

Consequences
The Beginning of Wisdom

"Sooner or later everybody has to sit down
to a banquet of consequences."

— Robert Louis Stevenson

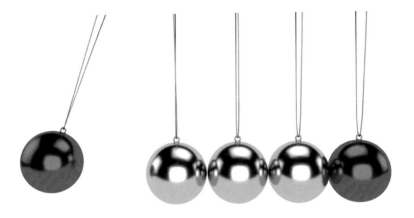

Satan works the extremes. He either entices us to choose
actions that bring devastating consequences or he tells us to
do whatever we want and there will be no consequences.

In physics it's known as Newton's Third Law:
For every action there is an equal and
opposite reaction.

In our journey to exaltation,
it's the Law of Consequences:
Every action must have at least one.

Consequences must be proportionate to actions,
whether they be rewards or punishments.

As our own agents, we choose, we act,
and we are responsible for what happens.

We progress by experiencing consequences.

We can help others <u>before</u> an action by
discussing risks, rewards, and punishments.

And we can help others <u>after</u> a consequence by
reinforcing positive actions or salving the wounds
of improper actions, and thus help them learn.

But intervening <u>between</u> action and
consequence interferes with agency.

A dictator became fed up with pests so he ordered a new program to get rid of rats, flies, mosquitoes and sparrows, the latter because they ate farmers' grain. What no one had noticed, or at least had not been willing to tell the brutal tyrant, was that sparrows find locusts a delicacy. Too late. Consequences quickly followed as locusts swarmed the country eating entire fields of grain. Three million sparrows were killed, but between 15 and 45 million people starved to death, a ratio of five-to-one at minimum.[1]

Because of the 1958 ecological-imbalanced Four Pests campaign of … Mao Zedong.

☙

Before proceeding with an action, a test experiment and a willingness to think about secondary happenings might be advised, such as the role of natural predators in the above example. But real-life consequences are always the true teachers.

If classroom instruction were all that was needed to learn and progress, we might as well have stayed in heaven. But our Father knew that we would never appreciate living in His presence if we didn't experience at least some of the same things He experienced as He progressed.

So no matter how many videos of Tiger Woods and other great golfers you may study, for example, you will fail on the golf course if you never take a driver in your hand and feel the consequence of whacking that little white ball. You will never become an expert surgeon if all you do is study textbooks and never touch a scalpel. And you will never be an organist if all you do is watch Richard Elliott play the Conference Center organ.

Consequences can in many cases be anticipated because of agency and truth. Elder D. Todd Christofferson explains:

> "If it were not for the reality of fixed and immutable truths, the gift of agency would be meaningless since we would never be able to foresee and intend the consequences of our actions."[2]

∾

Let's now look at several action-consequence settings.

The Natural Episode

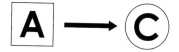

Justice demands that consequences *in some form* must always be felt. We will reap what we sow. That being in place, we can appreciate consequences as natural teachers: we act, we experience the results, we think about it, and we learn.

The consequence may be an *event* or a *process*. An <u>event</u>-consequence comes quickly. A <u>process</u>-consequence takes longer to unfold but is not never-ending. Letting it unfold is not a "serves you right" shot, but may well be the most compassionate thing to do because learning a lesson in life is always a positive. Examples:

> <u>Event</u>: An elementary school boy teases a girl to tears until her older brother hears about it. Let the consequence follow. One pop should be enough.

<u>Process</u>: A family member unwisely incurs a high-interest loan. Soon payment deadlines are missed and interest and penalties pile up. Relatives let the consequences proceed until the person slaps his forehead and vows, "I'll never do that again!" Dimpled chins and sloped foreheads can be good signs.

The Immediate Episode

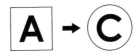

Here the action and the consequence are almost simultaneous. If you drop ferrous oxide into a beaker of hydrochloric acid, you will experience how fast you smell rotten egg gas. The olfactory senses teach a quick lesson in this case, but there is wisdom in a more prolonged wait between A and C.

President Spencer W. Kimball explained it:

> "If pain and sorrow and total punishment immediately followed the doing of evil, no soul would repeat a misdeed. If joy and peace and rewards were instantaneously given the doer of good, there could be no evil – all would do good and not because of the rightness of doing good. There would be no test of strength, no development of character, no growth of powers, no free agency only Satanic controls."[3]

Part of learning from our actions is reviewing what we just did *before* the full consequence kicks in. Deep down, we usually know quickly whether the action was a "Yes!" or an "Oops." Just as our whole time in mortality is a probationary period,[4] the space immediately after an action is its own *mini*-probationary period – a time to review, re-think, learn and savor or shun. It's critical we have time to think and be open to inspiration, rather than simply wait to be hit in the head or showered with "Attaboys." In other words, **let our self-ownership determine whether to do it again**, not simply be pushed this way or that by quick actual consequences.

The Delayed Episode

The natural man wants immediate rewards for good and delayed punishment for bad. While an immediate consequence may not be the best way of learning, a delayed consequence *may indeed* be the best way of learning. While criminals hope never to be discovered, many who are haunted by their crimes in time come to welcome being caught and paying their debt.

Then there are others who won't be around to be caught when the consequence comes due. Politicians who vote to borrow and spend today, intending to let future generations pay for it without enjoying the benefits, unrighteously act upon voters. They become kick-the-can-down-the-road puppeteers.

The Deep Episode

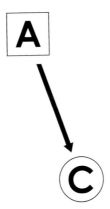

The story of the lost manuscript pages is instructive. When Joseph let Martin Harris take 116 pages home to show his wife, the Lord allowed Joseph his agency and **let the consequences sink in.** He did not intervene quickly to "make things all better" and then restore Joseph to the translation task. No, he let Joseph suffer regret and agony until he not only learned the lesson that came with the consequences, but more importantly became **determined** never to deviate from the Lord's instructions in the future.

"Young Joseph Smith was disciplined with a four-year probation before obtaining the golden plates," notes Elder Lynn G. Robbins. "Later, when Joseph lost the 116 manuscript pages, he was disciplined again. Though Joseph was truly remorseful, the Lord still withdrew his privileges for a short season …. Because the Lord wanted to teach Joseph a heart-changing lesson, He required a heartrending sacrifice of him – sacrifice being an essential part of discipline."[5]

The consequence that never seems to end is the most painful and yet the most lasting. "Learning a lesson the hard way" hasn't become a common phrase for no reason.

The Multiple Episode

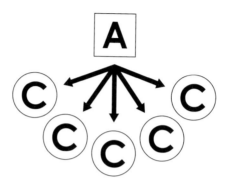

Though useful to analyze and learn from a single A-C episode, it is a rare act that doesn't have multiple consequences, good and/or bad.

I think it is safe to say that every act the Savior performed influenced more than one person. Whether it was feeding the 5000, obviously a multiple consequence event, or the healing of the woman who had faith to be cured if she could but touch His garment (the word spread), His every act had impact beyond one.

It's the nature of goodness. Though people may complain more than they compliment, and though evil is rampant, **the Savior is more capable of multiplying the impact of His disciples' good deeds than Satan is of multiplying evil ones.**

We are not to broadcast our service to others but help them quietly and without fanfare. But nothing stops the recipient from letting others know of a kindness, preferably without names, and thus goodness gets multiplied.

The Ripple Episode

Did the invention of air conditioning have anything to do with the election of Ronald Reagan as president?

As one author describes the ripple process, Willis Carrier invented air conditioning in Brooklyn which made industrial workplaces more comfortable and thus more productive. Workers returning to hot homes in the evening wondered why not make homes air conditioned, too. As costs came down, cooler homes increased. And then the thought, why not move to the south to escape cold winters and have reasonably comfort in the summer as well? The mass migration to the South turned a bloc of solid Democratic states into Republican states, changed electoral college calculations, and contributed to Reagan's 1980 victory.[6] Not the major reason for his victory, of course, but a good illustration of how inventors cannot possibly visualize the ripples and all the ways their inventions will impact the future.

Many times an action will have an ongoing impact (influence, consequence) on future generations even if the original action wasn't considered a big deal by the original actor. President James E. Faust told this story in the April 2001 General Conference:

"Many years ago an elder who served a mission in the British Isles said at the end of his labors, 'I think my mission has been a failure. I have labored all my days as a missionary here and I have only baptized one dirty little Irish kid. That is all I baptized.'

"Years later, after his return to his home in Montana, he had a visitor come to his door who asked, 'Are you the elder who served a mission in the British Isles in 1873?'

'Yes.'

"Then the man went on, 'And do you remember having said that you thought your mission was a failure because you had only baptized one dirty little Irish kid?'

"He said, 'Yes.'

"The visitor put out his hand and said, 'I would like to shake hands with you. My name is Charles A. Callis, of the Council of the Twelve of The Church of Jesus Christ of Latter-day Saints. I am that dirty little Irish kid that you baptized on your mission.'"[7]

President Faust continued: "Elder Callis ... blessed the lives of literally thousands. I feel privileged to have known this great Apostle of the Lord when I was a young man."

From seemingly small acts ....

The Reaction Episode

Life being complex, a consequence can follow an action, then become an action itself forcing a consequence on someone else, and so forth.

Baseball is a playful example:

> The pitcher acts in throwing the baseball, the hitter accepts the consequence of the ball coming toward him and acts in return by hitting it to the shortstop who receives the consequence in his glove and acts by throwing the baseball to the first baseman thus defeating the hitter.

The point is one action may produce not only a consequence but lead to a series of A-C episodes, some useful, some destructive, and some entertaining.

The False Connection

If poverty causes crime, does affluence cause honesty?

Government has assumed for decades that eliminating poverty would eliminate crime and has spent billions trying to prove it. Has it worked? Except for the promise that if we keep God's commandments we will prosper in the land, socio-economic status and degree of honesty in today's societal constructs and manipulations do not correlate. We have dishonest poor and dishonest rich because each individual, regardless of economic status, has agency.

Feeling the Consequence

The consequence of an action may come quickly or may unfold slowly, but the guiding question is: When have we learned the lesson sufficiently that the consequence has done its job? Much depends on whether the experience is positive or negative and our resulting feelings about those consequences:

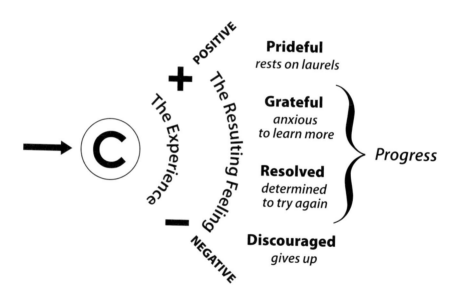

Not much progress is made by someone who is prideful about a good outcome or discouraged about a bad. We progress when we are grateful for a positive outcome, which excites us to learn more, or when a negative consequence prods the gritty among us to learn the lessons, cycle around and try again – rinse and repeat.

As one articulate cartoon character puts it, "D'oh."

Teach, Comfort, or Intervene?

A friend told me of a conversation he had with his daughter after she married and moved out. He asked, "How did I do?" She replied, "I wish you had let me feel more of the consequences of my actions."

What do you do when someone else is the actor and you are the observer, such as a parent? Three stages to consider:

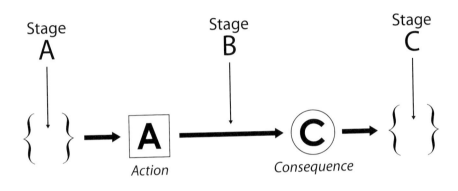

Helping someone at **Stage A** is *education* before the action. Over a long period, parents teach their children right and wrong and point out the rewards or punishments that await. In the shorter period, they act decisively to prevent injury or loss of life – e.g., babies who don't understand hot stoves or gravity.

Helping someone at **Stage C** is *compassion* and service, but only *after* a lesson has been learned. If the action was negative, we pick them up, dust them off, salve the wound, discuss what happened, and encourage them try again – wince and repeat, so to speak. If the action was positive, we reinforce the correctness of their choice and stand available to discuss the next steps in their journey.

Helping someone at **Stage B**, such as being a helicopter parent, usually backfires because it disconnects the natural sequence. If you step in to help before valuable lessons are taught by the consequences, you are postponing progress and will surely face the same situation again as the person will plead, "But you helped me last time." It's best if Stage B is considered a *no-trespassing zone.*

> Chicks should be left alone to break out of their shells by themselves. If someone intervenes to make it easier for them, they often don't survive.

Protect people from valuable consequences and they will become lazy, envious, and conniving: "How much can I get without doing anything?" They become scammers. Most of all, they don't learn the lessons our Father desires they learn.

"Our Heavenly Father is not a 'helicopter parent,'" explained Elder D. Todd Christofferson. "He does not generally intervene to protect us from the consequences of our choices. If He routinely acted that way, our cherished moral agency would become meaningless."[8]

Abortion is a prime example of intervening between action and consequence. Rarely justified, the effects ripple and the one undesired consequence is replaced by multiple others.

As noted in the Socialism chapter, politicians seeking votes and power intervene in a different way. The action is to promise and deliver "free stuff" but shift the consequence to future generations through deficit spending. The beneficiaries don't feel the pain and those who will feel it will not have received the benefit.

All such intervention plays into Satan's strategy to prevent consequences and thus thwart God's plan for our progress. He tasks his followers to mess with the consequences of our actions in three ways: (1) If it's a good action, prevent the rewards; (2) If it's a bad action, let damaging punishment flow; and (3) If it's a bad action from which something good might be learned, modify the consequences to increase damage and dilute learning.

The purpose in all three methods is to discourage actions that could lead to progress and improvement. When Satan whispers, "There's no harm in this" or "Nobody will know" or "Everybody's doing it," he's really saying there will be no consequences. Thus **if Satan can dilute, diminish, or destroy consequences, our learning is accordingly diluted, diminished, and destroyed**.

This is not to say all interventions are improper. Many stories tell of soldiers placing themselves between enemy guns and fellow warriors at the cost of their own lives. And of course if a baby crawls to the edge of a second-story balcony and falls, a passerby isn't going to let it bounce to teach it a lesson. We intervene against a consequence only if a greater good can be realized.

Satan's Subtle Scam: Consequence Shifting

Most actions have multiple consequences. If a woman thinks about having an abortion, for example, she will think about cost, pain and, we would hope, what happens in the hereafter if not repented of. Contemplating all consequences may prompt her to accept her actions and give birth to the baby. Satan, however, strengthens the temptation to abort by shifting one or more consequences, in this case having "someone else" pay for it. Once the cost of the abortion is shifted to the taxpayers, the woman may find it hard to turn down something that's free.

The reason more of us are not up in arms about such consequence shifting harks back to the adage that *the few who receive a lot will always care more than the many who each contribute a little.* Pro-abortion Planned Parenthood receives $500 million a year in government funding which means each American pays only $1.54 for their services while each woman receiving an abortion receives a "benefit" many times that.[9] Thus **morality is weakened as unwise government spending re-directs consequences** and decreases the woman's chances to learn and progress.

Satan's Big Scam: No Consequences

Most of us know intuitively that actions always bring commensurate rewards or punishments as justice demands, that the law of action-reaction cannot be ignored. It's obvious there must always be consequences.[10] But one ingenious manipulator argued that the action-consequence model can be made inoperative and convinced billions of God's children to believe his playbook and follow him.

Lucifer peddled the whopper that people could indulge their lusts however they wanted and he would guarantee they would all return to heaven. This "no consequences" enticement – this separation of consequences from actions – is such a siren song that it is referenced at least four times in the Book of Mormon:

- Nephi warned that "there shall also be many which shall say: Eat, drink, and be merry; nevertheless, fear God – he will justify in committing a little sin; yea, lie a little, take the advantage of one because of his words, dig a pit for thy neighbor; **there is no harm in this**; and do all these things, for tomorrow we die; and if it so be that we are guilty, God will beat us with a few stripes, and at last **we shall be saved** in the kingdom of God."[11]

- Moroni prophesied that "there shall be many who will say, Do this, or do that, and **it mattereth not**, for the Lord will uphold such at the last day."[12]

- Korihor, the anti-Christ, taught that "every man fared in this life according to the management of the creature; therefore every man prospered according to his genius, and that every man conquered according to his strength; and **whatsoever a man did was no crime.**"[13]

- Another Book of Mormon villain, Nehor, implied there would be no consequences to actions, no matter number or severity: "And he also testified unto the people that **all mankind should be saved** at the last day, and that they need not fear nor tremble, but that they might lift up their heads and rejoice; for the Lord had created all men, and had also redeemed all men; and, in the end, **all men should have eternal life.**"[14]

All four scenarios violate justice – that punishments must fit the crime and rewards must equal the deed. In these false promises, a life of riotous and lascivious living can be ignored or at most paid for with a few stripes.

The fact is, many welcome such no-consequences individuals and even heap honors on them.

> But behold, if a man shall come among you and shall say: Do this, and there is no iniquity; do that and ye shall not suffer ... ye will receive him, **and say that he is a prophet.**[15]

Consider as well the observation from a modern-day prophet, Elder Quentin L. Cook:

> "One of the unique and troubling aspects of our day is that many people engage in sinful conduct but refuse to consider it sinful. They have no remorse or willingness to acknowledge their conduct as being morally wrong. Even some who profess a belief in the Father and the Son *wrongfully take the position that a loving Father in heaven should exact no consequences* for conduct that is contrary to His commandments."[16]

No consequences, a guaranteed return ticket, an easy short cut, salvation without effort, something for nothing, risk-free sin. It definitely appealed to the lazy, the gullible, and the free-lunch crowd – billions of them.[17] Still does.

Satan knows that if agency is destroyed, God's plan for our salvation crumbles. Separating consequences from actions is his best chance to do it.

❦

"We are free to choose what we will and to pick and choose our acts, but we are not free to choose the consequences. They come as they will come."

– Boyd K. Packer

Chapter 21

Victimhood
"It's Not Fair" and
Other Fragrant Whines

"99% of failures come from people who make excuses."
– George Washington

Whiners complain about everything and appreciate nothing.
Victimhood has become so desirable that people look
for opportunities to be offended and thus
open themselves to demagoguery.

Contrary to conventional reasoning,
victimhood often begins when someone is rescued
from the consequences of an action.

The person is robbed of a learning experience
and its consequent weight of responsibility.

If continued, the person becomes irresponsible.

Accustomed to being rescued,
he becomes a pampered snowflake.

Demanding safe spaces and trigger warnings,
he insists society protect him from
opposition, discomfort, and misfortune.

When the unpleasant nonetheless happens,
he bemoans the unfairness and is
quick to blame others.

"It's not fair." "You failed me." "It's not my fault."

He relishes in victimhood
and thus becomes a patsy for ever-plentiful,
something-for-nothing schemes.

Most importantly, he refuses to use opposition as
the progress-producing instrument God intended.

Once upon a time, as the saying goes, a nation was in bondage to another. They were slaves put to hard labor digging, building huge monuments, and growing food for their masters. It continued for decades until one day they were miraculously rescued and allowed to flee the country.

Their rescuer led them across a sea, and they complained their feet got wet. As they traveled farther, they grumbled about lack of water. Food was provided, but they griped about its boring sameness.

They even reminisced on their slavery days and how good they had it, as they so selectively remembered. "We had meat, we had bread, and now we're going to starve to death in the wilderness." On and on, grumbling, griping, complaining, whining.

Victimhood was woven into them to such an extent that the rescuer had to wait for the old geezers to die off and the next generation to take a more promising view of their world and their future.

You know who I'm describing. With only a little embellishment … the Israelites Moses tried to help.

Victimhood has definitely been around awhile.

∽

So how does it tie to agency? At first glance, a chapter on victimhood appears but an amusing sidelight to our main topic. I maintain the two are seriously and intricately connected.

Victimhood Culture

A good example of an "it's-no-fair" whiner in the scriptures has to be Alma's son Corianton who had slipped away from his missionary duties to chase harlots in the land of Siron (succumbing to the original Siron song, perhaps?). He apparently argued that being punished for sin is unfair – a basic misunderstanding of the actions-have-consequences principle. Alma references his whine – "concerning the justice of God in the punishment of the sinner; for ye do try to suppose that it is injustice that the sinner should be consigned to a state of misery"[1] – and then lays out what I believe to be the most powerful exposition of sin, justice, atonement, repentance, and mercy found in the scriptures, Alma 42. Fortunately for Corianton, Alma's words turned him to repentance and he remained true.

Who are today's self-appointed victims? They're easy to spot. They...

- Identify others as the cause of undesired situations.
- Deny personal responsibility for their own life or circumstances.
- Look for reasons to feel offended.
- Believe others are more fortunate.
- Gain relief from receiving attention and empathy.
- Feel others are obligated to help them.[2]

That last point reminds me of the movie in which the village milkman gives the town beggar a kopeck. The beggar says, "One kopeck? Last week you gave me two kopeks." He replies that he had a bad week to which the beggar retorts, "So, if you had a bad week, why should I suffer?"[3]

That's pure victimhood and in ever-increasing numbers, the touchy and easily offended form the Victimhood Culture:

"I'm not responsible for what happened. It's not fair. It's somebody else's fault. I'm suffering. The world owes me. I deserve to be taken care of."

American colleges lead the charge. Many have established teams to investigate comments of students and professors – free speech, no less – that make others feel offended or even mildly uncomfortable. Reports of offensive speech include a roommate who was watching a video of a conservative commentator, a student who jokingly described herself

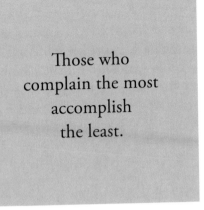

Those who complain the most accomplish the least.

being schizophrenic at times, a food-service worker saying hello in Japanese to an Asian-American student, and a student who complained about a professor who assigned too many classic works on economics written by men.[4]

Snowflakes on steroids banging spoons on their high chairs.

Criminals have the script down pat. A prison supervisor told me that over half of the violent inmates in his jurisdiction continue to claim they didn't do it, their convictions in courts of law notwithstanding. And most of those who *do* own up to the act point the finger at others – he called me a name, my marriage was going bad, I have a medical condition, they made me mad, he hit me first, it was self-defense, I was set up, I had bad parents, even "the coffee was cold." So creative.

Exploiting Scapegoats

Columnist Jim Geraghty notes:

"People seek scapegoats, and a lot of hate is seeking someone to blame. I'd argue the greatest antidote to hate in society is individual responsibility. If your life stinks, at least half of your problems are a result of decisions you've made. People loathe hearing this. Taking a hard look at your own past decisions, habits, excuses is probably one of the most difficult things to do in life. … It is much, much easier and more reassuring to conclude someone else caused your problems."[5]

The victim culture obviously blocks the individual's progress, but the victim's urge for a scapegoat also backfires, this time on society, because it invites exploiters to stir up faux sympathy to gain power, as we explored in the Socialism chapter:

"You poor thing. It IS someone else's fault. We'll show those bad guys. We'll tax the rich so you can have free stuff."

It's another form of disconnecting consequences from actions – a twist on the old "do whatever you want, you won't be held responsible" shtick. But this time it comes with goodies: because you're a victim, we'll force society to take care of you. **A delightful existence for one and a ticket to power for the other.**

> "The left celebrates victimhood over resilience and self-sufficiency."
>
> – Bobby Jindal

This *false* empathy hides an underlying goal (votes, power, a slice of the proceeds) while *true* empathy focuses on solving the underlying problem (self image, better employment, face reality, etc.), providing, meanwhile, only necessary food and resources until the person acknowledges his situation and stands on his own feet.

Intellectualism and those who gain power by playing to the victim mentality (by giving away free stuff) form a more serious abuse of agency: telling average people that they aren't smart enough or capable enough to decide things for themselves. They have become the string pullers warned against.

With all this deception, self-esteem suffers. Those who believe a robust view of self is based on what one <u>possesses</u> don't understand that true and healthy self-esteem can only be gained through <u>effort</u>.

A perceptive *Calvin & Hobbes* comic strip had Calvin complaining that a bad grade on his paper was lowering his self-esteem. The teacher responded, "Then you should work harder so you don't get bad grades." After a puzzled moment, Calvin replied, "Your denial of my victimhood is lowering my self-esteem."[6]

Victimhood – a core personality trait?

The Road to Atheism

The victimhood mentality is more serious than it first appears because it undermines a basic principle of agency and our existence:

If actions have consequences, there is justice.

If actions do not have consequences, there is no justice.

God is a god of justice.

So if justice is not, God ceases to be God.[7]

Couldn't be simpler.

Extend it. If a man acts improperly, how can he possibly repent if he never admits he made a mistake in the first place? And if he doesn't repent, how can he possibly expect mercy? Denying these connections, how can he possibly be a follower of Christ?

The more we follow Christ, the more willing we are to repent of mistakes instead of blaming others for misfortunes. Further,

the more we follow Christ, the more we realize that <u>opposition in all things is necessary for progress</u>. The whiner does not have such attitudes.

Just the opposite. **The whining victim hood finds it easier to rationalize his actions if he convinces himself there is no God to answer to.** Ergo, no accountability. We could even go so far as to say those who deny their mistakes are on the **road to atheism**.[8]

Impact of Victim Hoods on Society

Social justice warriors agitate for equality in the distribution of resources, wealth, and privileges. They want a new type of mercy, **a forgiveness in the form of entitlement**.

Of course we want everyone to share in the world's resources, but we must do so by equality of opportunity, not the force of equal outcomes. When someone receives an entitlement disproportionate to effort, even a rudimentary understanding of human behavior concludes it...

- Fosters a mentality that consequences can be avoided.

- Causes onlookers to be less willing to serve others out of magnanimity.

- Works against agency's commandment that we act.

- Discourages individual initiative.

- Desensitizes people to those suffering real problems.

- Divides society into competing attitudes about work.

- Decreases a society's productivity.

- Freezes effort and risk taking.

A healthy society must allow consequences and its citizens must stifle the urge to whine and shift blame. Otherwise it drifts to anarchy. Sooner or later, that society must blow the whistle on the whiners and their microaggressions, safe spaces, trigger warnings, emotional well-being violations, fixations on hate speech, and unlimited claims of discrimination. Enablers, as with busybodies, must be opposed if only for the benefit of those watching from the sidelines.

> "This means some of us won't make it back to live with the Father. No fair."
>
> – Someone in the pre-earthly existence

Those who revel being a victim fail to appreciate the magnificent gift of agency and forfeit the progress they could have made.

Blaming others, notes Elder Dale G. Renlund. "allows us to excuse our behavior. By so doing, we shift responsibility for our actions to others. When the responsibility is shifted, we diminish both the need and our ability to act. We turn ourselves into hapless victims rather than agents capable of independent action."[9]

❧

"By and large, I have come to see that if we complain about life, it is because we are thinking only of ourselves."
— Gordon B. Hinckley

Chapter 22

Responsibility
More Than Facing the Music

"The opportunity to assume personal responsibility is a
God-given gift without which we cannot realize our
full potential as daughters and sons of God."
— D. Todd Christofferson

We received the gift of responsibility – a sub-gift of agency –
when we became self-existing, conscious spirit children of God.
With it came our agreement to be accountable before Him for
our actions. Perfection can come through no other process.

Responsibility is attached to
every choice and action.

But there's a difference between
having responsibility, which is automatic, and
being responsible, which is a choice.

The phrase "he is responsible" can mean
the person carries the burden for the consequences
or the person has character.

If we acknowledge our responsibility,
we become responsible and
build within ourselves honorable character.

If we avoid responsibility, however,
we lack character, we violate God's gift,
and our progress suffers.

Responsibility leads to accountability and
one day we will be answerable for our actions.

We may share responsibility,
but accountability will be ours alone.

On the fateful morning of September 11, 2001, United flight 93 took off from Newark bound for California. Somewhere over Ohio, terrorists hijacked the plane and turned it toward Washington, D.C.

A few passengers, talking to family on the ground, heard of the other airliner hijackings that day and quickly figured out they were heading for a similar fate. They decided to do something about it.

Passenger Thomas Burnett, Jr., told his wife over the phone: "I know we're all going to die. There's three of us who are going to do something." And then another passenger, Todd Beamer, was heard saying, "Are you guys ready? Let's roll."[1]

As they fought the hijackers in the cockpit, the plane flipped over and crashed at high speed in western Pennsylvania. Though all on board lost their lives, those who acted saved many others.

They took responsibility. They acted.

❧

Let's sort out the related words.

Responsibility is a <u>condition, a possession</u>. We automatically assumed a lifelong mantle of responsibility for our actions before we came to earth. It means…

- ✔ We have authority over ourselves; we are not only our own owners, we are our own <u>leaders</u>.

- ✔ We can be given <u>stewardships</u> – authority over resources or assignments for which we will report to the Giver.

- ✔ We can <u>progress</u> because it connects our actions to consequences, which are teachers.

- ✔ We must one day be accountable – **answerable** – for our actions.

As Stephen Covey phrased it: "The key is taking responsibility and initiative, deciding what your life is about and prioritizing your life around the most important things."

Responsible is a trait, a choice. It is a double-edged word based on actions: "Okay, who's responsible for this mess?" and "I would like to thank those responsible for this wonderful banquet." On the one hand it teams with finger pointing as a word of blame. On the positive side, we associate it with character and service, with accomplishing good, and points to someone who is to be thanked or rewarded.

The phrase "he is responsible" means the person carries the burden for the consequences or the person has character. Being responsible is *not a passive trait; it connotes action.*

"Man must cease attributing his problems to his environment," Albert Schweitzer said, "and learn again to exercise his will – his personal responsibility in the realm of faith and morals."

Responsibly is a description. Acting responsibly…

- ✔ Causes us to accomplish things and gives us courage to continue to act and do;

- ✔ Signals people they can trust us, which in turn leads to leadership opportunities; and

- ✔ Builds self-confidence and leads to the capacity to endure to the end.

That last point is critical. Because taking responsibility builds self-confidence, we feel strong, we have self-reliance. Because we face challenges and take responsibility for consequences, we have more confidence to face whatever the future dishes out. We become confident of making it to the end; we have **endurance**. On the other hand, those who fail to act responsibly become weak because they spend their time thinking of excuses rather than learning and growing.

Responsibleness is the <u>sum total</u> of the previous three concepts. It is a quality intricately <u>connected to freedom</u>. Viktor Frankl advised: "Freedom ... is in danger of degenerating into mere arbitrariness unless it is lived in terms of responsibleness. That is why I recommend that the Statue of Liberty on the East Coast be supplemented by a Statue of Responsibility on the West Coast."

> "Responsibility is a unique concept ... You may share it with others, but your portion is not diminished."
>
> – Hyman Rickover

Counterintuitive as it may appear, **responsibility doesn't shackle, it liberates.**

Belonging Takes the Cake

At times people want more responsibility than they're given.

Powdered eggs were invented in the 1930s. After their use in GI rations in World War II, General Mills created a line of cake mixes in the 1950s that included eggs and milk in powder form to make cake-baking easier for American moms. Simply add water, mix and bake. What's not to like? Families would get a great treat and homemakers would save time. Under the well-known Betty Crocker brand, the cake mix seemed a shoo-in. But it bombed.

Call in the psychologists with the focus groups.

They found that a mother baked a cake as a sign of her love and the drudgery of traditional cake-baking was the price she willingly paid. The General Mills cake mix took away responsibility and caused feelings of guilt by making it too easy. The mom in the family felt less involved and undeserving of credit.

Armed with this insight, the foodies then changed the recipe to let the homemaker add the eggs and a bit of oil, a formula that exists to this day. She became responsible for doing more than simply adding water. She now "owned" the cake and wasn't slipping by on her responsibility to provide that symbol of love.[2]

The point: time savers can backfire if they eliminate a responsibility people may need for involvement and self-esteem. It gets back to agency and self-ownership – that acting responsibly means "I'm important; I'm part of life; I can make a difference."

And Then Comes Accountability

"Agency and accountability are eternal principles. We exercise our free agency not only by what we do, but also by what we decide, or will, or desire. Restrictions on freedom can deprive us of the power to do, but no one can deprive us of the power to will or desire. **Accountability must therefore reach and attach consequences to the desires of our hearts.**"[3] – Dallin H. Oaks

Accountability runs parallel with responsibility and we will be accountable both for what we did and what we failed to do with our agency. The scriptures are firm:

That every man may act ... according to the moral agency which I have given unto him, that every man may be **accountable for his own sins** in the day of judgment.[4]

[Y]e must all stand before the judgment-seat of Christ, yea, every soul who belongs to the whole human family of Adam; and ye must stand to be **judged of your works**, whether they be good or evil.[5]

[F]or it is required of the Lord, at the hand of every steward, to **render an account** of his stewardship, both in time and in eternity.[6]

... every man shall be made accountable unto me ....[7]

Some think responsibility and accountability are the same. They are not.

- Responsibility functions before, during, and after an action. We receive reward or blame accordingly.

- Accountability only comes into play after an action. We alone are answerable for our actions, whether with others or not.

- **Responsibility can be shared; accountability cannot.**

We all know the day will come when we must stand before the Father and the Savior and answer for our actions. If we do not wish to be held accountable for a particular act, repentance is available, and all of us will have had sufficient teaching on the matter and opportunity to do so. But if we have disregarded the opportunity to plea for the Savior's grace and mercy, the time to say "please cut me some slack" has passed. Final measuring sticks are final measuring sticks.

Just before the onset of the order of Nehor, the Nephites ended the reign of kings and committed to being governed by the voice of the people.

"Think of three things: whence you came, where you are going, and to whom you must account."

– Benjamin Franklin

Therefore they relinquished their desires for a king, and became exceedingly anxious that every man should have an equal chance throughout all the land; yea, and every man expressed a **willingness to answer for his own sins**.[8]

Note the interplay: (1) rejection of power residing in one man – the structure of judges having just been given by Mosiah; (2) equal chance; (3) acceptance of accountability.

Democracy, equality, accountability. Each needs the others.

Accountable to Rules That Don't Change

Speaking at a convention of the American Baseball Coaches Association, John Scolinos, retired baseball coach at Cal Poly Pomona, explained the permanence and finality of certain things in his sport and drew parallels to life. He spoke for 25 minutes without ever mentioning a full-sized, stark-white home plate hanging from a string around his neck.

Then, as reported by a baseball consultant in the audience …

"You're probably wondering why I'm wearing home plate around my neck. … The reason I stand before you today is to share with you baseball people what I've learned in my life, what I've learned about home plate in my 78 years."

"Do you know how wide home plate is in Little League?" After a pause, someone offered, "Seventeen inches," more question than answer. …

"How wide is home plate in high school baseball?"

"Seventeen inches," they said, sounding more confident.

"And you college coaches, how wide is home plate in college?"

"Seventeen inches," we said in unison.

"Any Minor League coaches here? How wide is home plate in pro ball?"

"Seventeen inches!"

"RIGHT! And in the Major Leagues, how wide is home plate in the Major Leagues?"

"Seventeen inches!"

"SEV-EN-TEEN INCHES!" he confirmed, his voice bellowing off the walls. "And what do they do with a Big League pitcher who can't throw the ball over [a seventeen-inch plate]? ... "They don't say, 'Ah, that's okay, Jimmy. You can't hit a seventeen-inch target? We'll make it eighteen inches, or nineteen inches. We'll make it twenty inches so you have a better chance of hitting it. If you can't hit that, let us know so we can make it wider still, say twenty-five inches.'"

Pause. "Coaches ..." *Pause.*

"... what do we do when our best player shows up late to practice? When our team rules forbid facial hair and a guy shows up unshaven? What if he gets caught drinking? **Do we hold him accountable? Or do we change the rules to fit him?**

"*Do we widen home plate?*"[9]

Just as baseball has its seventeen-inch wide plate, so too our life and God's requirements of us. We are taught the widths of the plates – the commandments.

The widths of the Father's "home plates" have never changed and never will.

President Wilford Woodruff:

"By virtue of ... agency, you and I and all mankind are made responsible beings, responsible for the course we pursue, for the lives we live, the deeds we do in the body."[10]

❧

"We have the agency to make choices, but ultimately we will be accountable for each choice we make."

– James E. Faust

Chapter 23

Experience
Learning From Mistakes

"Character cannot be developed in ease and quiet.
Only through experience of trial and suffering can the soul be
strengthened, ambition inspired, and success achieved."
– Helen Keller

"It is necessary," President John Taylor stated, " … that we pass
through the school of suffering, trial, affliction, and privation,
to know ourselves, to know others, and to know our God."[1]

The verb most associated with
the noun experience is gain.

We think, we choose, we act ...
and we gain experience.

But we will not enjoy the
fruits of experience unless ...

We are completely involved in and
have full ownership of our actions.

We reflect deeply upon our actions
after we have felt the consequences.

We make turns and changes in our life
to align us with the path to exaltation.

We recognize the need for tribulation
so we can better appreciate the good.

Exaltation is unreachable without experience.

Remember the story of US Airways Captain Chesley "Sully" Sullenberger and his Hudson River landing in January 2009? Shortly after taking off from LaGuardia airport, a flock of geese hit his Airbus A320 snuffing out power in both engines. Realizing he could not return to LaGuardia or reach any other airport, he lined up an approach to the Hudson River. I doubt he was thinking "Now do I want an x-degree or a y-degree approach angle?" No, he handled the whole thing by "feel" and here is where his experience came in. He not only had thousands of hours in jet aircraft, but also considerable time flying … gliders. Pilots tell us there is a difference between a powered landing and a glider landing, and Sully had just the right experience, just the right feel for his jet-turned-glider. Analysts estimated that if the angle of his plane had been slightly higher or slightly lower, it would have cartwheeled as it hit the water and lives would have been lost. But by the feel of experience he threaded it to a perfect landing.

He later said, "One way of looking at this might be that for 42 years, I've been making small, regular deposits in this *bank of experience*, education and training. And on January 15, the balance was sufficient so that I could make a very large withdrawal."[2]

Experience – the little deposits of life.

☙

Experience and the Power of Mistakes

[All] these things shall give thee **experience**, and shall **be for thy good**.[3]

Thus the Lord's conclusion after stepping the Prophet Joseph through 15 what-ifs ranging from robbers to billowing surges to the very jaws of hell gaped open. That is, no matter the severity or number of trials, every single experience we suffer shall be for our good. Wow! Looked at from another angle, the success of agency is often hidden in trials and struggles, things a short-term oriented world wants to prevent.

As stated before, this world was designed so things **will** go wrong. How else are we to learn? When we feel the consequences of our actions, we learn. And the most painful ones are often our best teachers. No mistakes, no learning.

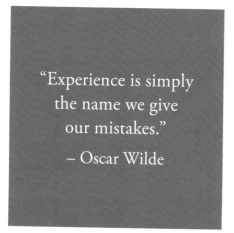

"Experience is simply the name we give our mistakes."

– Oscar Wilde

Of course, we don't have to make all the mistakes the world has made to experience life. We should learn from the mistakes of others and build on them by making **new** mistakes – the ones they would have made had they lived long enough. Progress comes from finding new actions, the consequences of which give us experience, learning, and ultimately wisdom.

We can <u>have an experience</u> without necessarily <u>gaining experience</u>. The difference is how we handle it. If it's a good experience, do we treasure it and build upon it to strengthen personal qualities, thanking God for the opportunity, ... or do we consider it our just due and smugly remain oblivious? If it's a bad experience, do we learn from it and commit to do better, or do we whine, blame others, and retreat into a selfish cocoon?

We should also remember that the fruits of agency are often long-term rather than short-term. Progress may depend on suffering today so we become productive tomorrow.

Heavenly Father wants us to become perfect as He is. He does this not by micromanaging every detail of our behavior, but by giving us eternal principles by which we can *learn* to become perfect. And we become such step by step by making mistakes. When we learn something for ourselves by our own experience, it sticks. If someone tells us and compels us, it doesn't.

Learning from mistakes makes us self-governing.

No Experience Without Experiencing Experiences

Picture this. God has created worlds without number and people without number. If each of those children had a minimal number of experiences, would there be any events, episodes, or experiences that no one has *ever* had? Any that have never ever happened on one world or another throughout the eons of space and time? Except for the Savior's Atonement and resurrection, are there any events on this earth that haven't already happened elsewhere? Doubtful.

And isn't it logical that somewhere along the line, in whatever languages, those stories have been written down?

So why not make them available in some grand celestial library or iCloud? We could read them, learn from them, and absorb the collective wisdom of billions. No need for our own mortal existence.

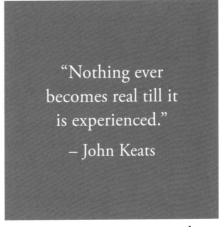

"Nothing ever becomes real till it is experienced."

– John Keats

Read about the mistakes of others, promise not to repeat them, and ta-da … exaltation.

But somehow it doesn't seem logical that experiences can be experienced without being experienced.

Look at it this way. Would you learn more from a teacher who tells you about others who have climbed Mt. Everest, or from someone who has actually climbed it? And wouldn't you learn even more if you personally climbed it?

And so it is. We cannot become perfect by reading or listening to lectures. We must be fully **involved** with our chosen steps in life and shoulder full ownership to really learn. We must personally **feel** an action as it unfolds and then **feel** the consequences when they inevitably hit us. No story about someone else, however fascinatingly written, can match it. Or teach it.

> On the first Sunday of the month, some people fast and others just go hungry. They each learn different things from their experience.

Agency optimizes choices. The more the choices, the greater the opportunities to experiment. The more we experiment, the more the failures. The more the failures, the more we appreciate success when it happens. The more we appreciate what we learn by trial and error, the more we progress.

Failures – Stepping Stones to Success

Why do people flock to see the Leaning Tower of Pisa? If it were straight, it would be just another ho-hum. We are fascinated with failures because we know we too will fail, but that good can result.

The stories about failures being precursors to success are legion.

Walt Disney was fired by a newspaper because he lacked imagination and had no good ideas. His first studio went bankrupt and he couldn't find distribution for the first Mickey Mouse features.

The first two Wright Brothers' flight experiments failed. Same with Milton Hershey and his first three candy ventures. Steven Spielberg had poor grades in high school and the University of Southern California turned him down three times.

Abraham Lincoln lost eight political races for various offices before landing the big one. Charles Schultz's drawings were rejected by his high school yearbook. Colonel Sanders, a 6th grade dropout, tried selling his secret fried chicken recipe and was rejected a thousand times.

As a sophomore, Michael Jordan was cut from his high school basketball team. He began putting in more practice time and eventually could say, "I've failed over and over and over again in my life. And that is why I succeed."

And Abraham Lincoln could say, "My great concern is not whether you have failed, but whether you are content with your failure."

Toss in Henry Ford: "Failure is the opportunity to begin again more intelligently."

George Washington is a special example. He fought many battles in the dead of winter and once had to swim to safety in a freezing river. While fighting malaria, he lost a third of his soldiers in a battle. He and his men suffered from lack of supplies and he camped with his men in the cold instead of living in warmer quarters like others of his rank. States promised him more recruits but never lived up to their promises.

Through it all, he kept his forces together while being pursued across New York and New Jersey and suffering defeats in battle. After crossing the Delaware on Christmas night of 1776, and his subsequent victories at Trenton and Princeton, he went almost five years without another one until Cornwallis was cornered at Yorktown.[4]

Here was a man the Lord chose to play a critical role in the founding of America. Some may wonder why He didn't do more to smooth the way. Well, He didn't because the tough events Washington went through gave him the experience he needed to resist the urge to become a monarch but rather be the first president of the first nation to declare the people sovereign over government, and prepare the land designated to host the restoration of the gospel.

Tribulation is necessary for advancement.

Reflection – Thinking Deeply to Learn

First man: "If someone told you to jump off a bridge, would you do it?"

Second man thinking deeply: "Well, not again."

"What happened back there?" should be the question after every action, even before consequences are felt. It's ponder power again, the wondering what we could have done differently to achieve a better outcome. Reflection can be the reason our worst experiences can lead to our greatest progress.

In what was probably less than two hours, Peter denied the Savior three times. Realizing he had just fulfilled the Savior's prophecy, "... Peter went out, and wept bitterly."[5] He thought deeply, decided what to do, and then went unwaveringly forward to become the fearless and unapologetic leader of The Church of Jesus Christ of Early-day Saints.

Reflection requires patience. Paul tells us in Romans "... we glory in tribulations also: knowing that tribulation worketh patience; and patience, experience; and experience, hope."[6] And later in the epistle to be "patient in tribulation."[7]

The more we patiently think about and ponder on our actions and especially the consequences, the wiser will be our future actions and the less our wasted time.

Repentance – The Enhancer of Experience

If upon reflecting on an action you see how to improve and you act on that insight, congratulations – you have just marshaled the power of the "Great Enhancer."

Contrary to its image, repentance is not a punishment and it's more than saying "Sorry." It is a power, a clarifier, an amplifier of doctrine. It's the opportunity to use consequences to maximize learning and deepen wisdom.

The word for repentance in Hebrew is *teshuva*, which means to turn or return – that is, to turn away from a past behavior toward a better one. Like the man who felt a need to repent because he was addicted to the hokey pokey, so ... he turned himself around.

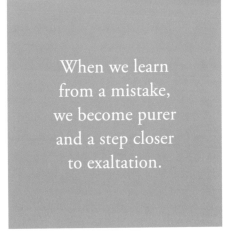

When we learn from a mistake, we become purer and a step closer to exaltation.

He added, "That's what it's all about."

To turn means to act: "... **turn** to God and **do** works meet for repentance."[8] It relates to the ultimate goal of agency because no mortal has ever trod a straight path to exaltation. Our lives take twists and turns and every turn is a point of *change*, which incidentally is the Greek word for repentance (*metaneoeo* meaning change of air or spirit). Whether turn or change, either is better than the harsh word repent, which is based on the Latin root that also gave us penalty, penitentiary, and punishment.

Ignore the unfortunate translation and focus on the original teaching. This change in attitude (spirit) and turn in a better direction helps us to ...

See more clearly what has happened;

Maximize what we learn from our actions;

Readjust our strategy;

Get back on the strait and narrow; and

Better align ourselves with God's plan for us.

On the other hand, if we ignore the need to change (refuse to repent), we're doomed to make the same mistakes again. Stupidity, as they say, is doing the same thing over and over and expecting a different outcome. "Don't get stuck on stupid," goes a favorite saying in some quarters.

> **When our life's record is presented in the courts above, won't we hope our repentance was sufficient to produce a redacted version?**

Repentance not only enhances our learning and wisdom, but also our daily living conditions: "... and inasmuch as they did **repent** they did begin to **prosper**."[9] And it cleanses the mind: "And be not conformed to this world: but be ye transformed by the **renewing** of your mind ...."[10] Those little glial cells prune improper neuron connections and thus enervate neurons and dendrites to find new connections – hence inspiration and innovation.

As the bishop said to the workers who put too much thinner in the paint and botched his office renovation, "Repaint and thin no more."

The goal through our trials is to gather _experiences_ so we become _experienced_, capable of learning, advancing and accomplishing even more. An act or event will remain just a footnote in our life unless it prods us to change, turn, and act – wash, rinse, and try again.

President Dallin H. Oaks summed it up: "The purpose of God's plan was to give His children the opportunity to choose eternal life. This could be accomplished only by experience in mortality and, after death, by post-mortal growth in the spirit world."[11]

❧

"We are here on earth to gain experience we can obtain in no other way. ... How we face challenges and resolve difficult problems is crucially important to our happiness."
– Richard G. Scott

Chapter 24

Exaltation
Beyond Our Imagination

"Exaltation is our goal; discipleship is our journey."
– Dieter F. Uchtdorf

The gift of agency is the gift of exaltation,
conditioned upon obedience.

It's that simple.

The more fully we honor agency
empowered by the Savior's Atonement ...

The more insightful our thoughts,

The greater the power to discern truth and error,

The more proper the actions,

The greater the learning experiences,

The more willing the acceptance of accountability,

The purer the life and more sure the progress,

And the sooner we reach the goal
God desires for us ...

Exaltation

A man sits in a palace and must decide who makes it to the top. Heady stuff. He thinks about who has the right character- istics, who has led the right kind of life, how he gets along with others, who will persevere, the conditions surrounding the effort, and so on. A powerful official's dream.

So who is this heavy-duty judge?

We don't know his name, but he occupies an office in the Singha Durbar (Lion's Palace) government complex in Kathmandu, Nepal.

He decides who gets a permit to climb to the top of the world … Mt. Everest.

Top of the world. Let's compare it to the top of creation – exaltation.

	Mt. Everest	Exaltation
Who	Not everyone can be accommodated; only a few have a chance.	Everyone in the pre-mortal existence who chose to follow the Savior.
Qualifications	Healthy, strong, stamina, money	Keeps the commandments, repents of sins
Conditions to face	Snow, ice, wind, cold	Tribulations, trials, sorrows, pain
Competition	Every other mountain climber in the world	No one
Time	Less than 30 days a year, usually in May	Any time
Number	About 800 annually	Any number
How long stay on top	15 minutes if you're lucky	Forever
Judge	Permit grantor	Heavenly Father

The Life God Lives

A succinct definition of exaltation from the Gospel Principles manual:

"Exaltation is eternal life, the kind of life God lives. He lives in great glory. He is perfect. He possesses all knowledge and all wisdom. He is the Father of spirit children. He is a creator. We can become like our Heavenly Father. This is exaltation."[1]

What will life in the highest degree of the celestial kingdom be like? Let's look at three features we know about.

Presence

[T]hey who are just men made perfect through Jesus the mediator of the new covenant ... shall **dwell in the presence** of God and his Christ forever and ever.[2]

I once interviewed President Spencer W. Kimball on the grounds of the St. George temple for a Salt Lake TV station. I did a lousy job. Part of the reason was he made me feel comfortable and I was so absorbed being in his company that my client's goals became secondary. If he had asked me to drive him back to Salt Lake, I would have told my wife, Jan, to take the kids home and I'd catch up with her in a few days.

If members like me can feel that way in the presence of a prophet, how will we feel in the presence of God and His Son

… forever? It will be the fullness of joy and we will be "glorified and beautified beyond description,"[3] just as they are.

Power

Those found worthy of exaltation …

> … shall inherit thrones, kingdoms, principalities, and powers, dominions, all heights and depths … and a continuation of the seeds forever and ever. Then shall they be gods, because they have no end … because all things are subject unto them … because **they have all power** ….[4]

> Be ye therefore perfect, even as your Father which is in heaven is perfect.

The world has a jolly time mocking us on those verses – that God's children can themselves become gods, have the matter of the universe subject to them, live with members of their righteous family, and have children forever.

But I ask the mockers: What parents would not want their children to become as they are? **Why wouldn't our Heavenly Parents with their infinite love not want infinite joy for their infinite children?**

President Brigham Young stated that the power of eternal increase is the very purpose of the creation:

> "The whole object of the creation of this world is to exalt the intelligences that are placed upon it, that they may live, endure, and increase for ever and ever."[5]

Progress

People sometimes confuse progress and perfection. If God is perfect, they reason, why the principle of eternal progress?

Many fail to realize progress is not a single phase activity – perfect and done, sit back and relax. Rather, progress has at least two phases: (1) progress **toward perfection**, and then (2) progress in **applying perfection** such as creating and peopling worlds. Being perfect doesn't mean all progress has stopped; it only means one type of progress has been achieved and the second type now invites.

> "No one is granted power to prevent your exaltation. Only you can forfeit eternal life."
>
> – D. Todd Christofferson

Reaching the end goal of the first type of progress isn't going to happen here on earth; our full development will take a long time after we pass to the other side, as the Prophet Joseph Smith made clear:

> "When you climb up a ladder, you must begin at the bottom, and ascend step by step, until you arrive at the top; and so it is with the principles of the gospel – you must begin with the first, and go on until you learn all the **principles of exaltation**. But it will be **a great while** after you have passed through the veil [died] before you will have learned them. **It is not all to be comprehended in this world**; it will be a great work to learn our salvation and exaltation even beyond the grave."[6]

Note the emphasis on **learning** the principles of exaltation. And some think heaven is sitting on clouds playing harps.

Then comes progress phase two, basically unlimited. God told Moses that "**worlds without number** have I created" and then elaborated: [7]

> ... and by the Son I created them, which is mine Only Begotten.

> ... there are many worlds that have passed away by the word of my power. And there are many that now stand ...

> ... and innumerable are they unto man ...

> ... but all things are numbered unto me, for they are mine and I know them.

> The heavens, they are many, and they cannot be numbered unto man; but they are numbered unto me, for they are mine.

> And as one earth shall pass away, and the heavens therefore even so shall another come; and there is no end to my works, neither to my words.

It boggles the mind as we try to grasp the infinite nature of His creations and His counsel.

Purpose

In one of the most powerful, insightful, and hopeful of scriptures, God proclaimed His purpose: "For behold, this is my work and my glory – **to bring to pass the immortality and eternal life of man.**"

Think what that means. If we truly honor God's magnificent gift of agency, there will be one sure and inevitable outcome. No limited number of vacancies in the realms of exaltation and no end to the creations yet to be! Words are puny when contemplating it all. As even Shakespeare put it, "The best is yet to come."

In short, exaltation is to be as God is, know what He knows, inherit all He has, do what He does, and create as He creates. And He undoubtedly reserves unseen dimensions of exaltation yet to unfold.

Eye hath not seen, nor ear heard, neither have entered into the heart of man, the things which God hath prepared for them that love him.[8]

❧

If you keep my commandments and
endure to the end you shall have eternal life,
which gift is the greatest of all the gifts of God.[9]

Acknowledgements

Special thanks to …

My wife Jan for her love, support, encouragement, and especially her patience when I wrestled with writer's block.

My daughter Stephanie Smith for creating the cover design, designing the charts, graphs, and diagrams; editing; and doing the innovative layout – this while homeschooling her children, flipping houses, and serving as Relief Society president.

My assistant Colleen Arrington for legal and marketing logistics.

And thanks to all who contributed ideas, corrections, insights, and support, among them …

Merrilee Boyack
Greg Christofferson
Larry Eastland
John Evans
Tibor Farkas
Greg Fisher
LaRue and Dixie Frey
Shellie Frey
Robert Gardner
Glen Greener
Steve Hanson
Tony Hatch
Myrna Lea Houston
Bruce and Melody Hughes
Bryce Johnson
Ralph and Shauna Johnson
John Killpack
Jim Kinney

Kristen Lawrence
Woody Loveridge
Bart Marcois
Lindsey and Ben Miller
Barbara Openshaw
Warren Owens
Mary Kay Peirce
Oleg Popov
Maurine Proctor
Peter Rancie
Heather Richardson
Bud Scruggs
Mark Skousen
Ben Smith
Keith and Ira Stein
Brian Thomassen
Vernon and Sonja Wilbert
Hal and Colleen Williams

Stories

Quotes

A

Aristotle: 28, 233

B

Bach, Johann Sebastian: 113, 115
Ballard, M. Russell: 75, 107, 199
Bastiat, Frederic: 246
Bednar, David A.: 4, 19, 74, 145, 153, 157, 277
Beecher, Henry Ward: 114
Benson, Ezra Taft: 206, 258
Bonhoeffer, Dietrich: 116
Bradford, William: 253

C

Callister, Tad R.: 94
Carnegie, Andrew: 131
Castro, Martin: 198
Chesterton, G. K.: 175
Christensen, Clayton: 124, 229
Christofferson, D. Todd: 7, 21, 152, 284, 294, 309, 338
Churchill, Winston: 186
Cicero: 11
Clark, J. Reuben: 213
Confucius: 116
Cook, Quentin L.: 116, 162, 177, 192, 199, 297
Coolidge, Calvin: 205, 211, 230
Covey, Stephen: 311

D

Da Vinci, Leonardo: 31, 109, 114
De Tocqueville, Alexis: 215
Declaration of Independence: 213
Descartes: 113
Dickens, Charles: 174
Douglass, Frederick: 14

E

Edison, Thomas A.: 41, 114, 116, 119
Einstein, Albert: 29, 39
Emerson, Ralph Waldo; 116
Epstein, Joseph: 244
Etchemendy, John: 167

F

Faust, James E.: 83, 145, 153, 289, 318
Ford, Henry: 121, 325
Frankl, Viktor: 53
Franklin, Benjamin: 21, 315
Friedman, Milton: 20, 129, 134, 204, 209, 226, 227
Fry, Jeffrey: 123

G

Galileo: 114, 115
Gandhi: 115
George, Francis Cardinal: 175

Topics and Concepts

Notes

Introduction – The Gift

▢ Image: amasterphotographer/Shutterstock.com

1 Moses 6:55-56

2 *Atonement, Agency, Accountability*, Ensign, May 1988

3 2 Nephi 2:26

4 David A. Bednar, "Being an Agent to Act", https://www.lds.org/media-library/video/2016-03-0019-being-an-agent-to-act?lang=eng

5 https://www.prb.org/howmanypeoplehaveeverlivedonearth/ Moses 4:6 says Satan drew away many after him and we commonly assume from D&C 29:36 that this amounted to one-third of the hosts of heaven. But the phrase is "a third part of the hosts of heaven turned he away from me because of their agency." This third part could be a fraction or it could be a group. If the latter, then what are the first two groups? Are they the Lord's numbered sheep and those who are not numbered but also chose to follow the Father's plan? Or are the two groups those who chose to enter mortality and those who decided to remain in a spiritual state in heaven forever? We don't know. My point in any case is that the Father paid a steep price for our agency.

6 Church News, May 26, 2019, 10

Chapter 1 – Freedom

▢ Image: cla78/Shutterstock.com

1 https://en.wikipedia.org/wiki/Harriet_Tubman

2 Letter to James A. Bennett, Nauvoo, 8 September 1842

3 Alma 42:7

4 2 Corinthians 3:17

5 Eleventh Article of Faith

6 David A. Bednar, April 2010 General Conference

7 2 Nephi 2:27

8 D&C 98:8

9 2 Nephi 10:23

10 Helaman 14:30

11 Alma 61:15

12 BYU Devotional, December 12, 2017

Chapter 2 – Think

▢ Image: iStock.com/bestdesigns

1 https://en.wikipedia.org/wiki/Philo_Farnsworth

2 https://www.dw.com/en/new-images-prove-the-dendrites-in-your-brain-are-as-powerful-as-mini-computers/a-17188236

3 For an insightful discussion of this process, see The Enchanted Mind http://www.enchantedmind.com/html/science/quantum_brain.html

4 https://www.nature.com/news/snapshots-explore-einstein-s-unusual-brain-1.11836

5 https://en.wikipedia.org/wiki/Einstein%27s_thought_experiments. Also: http://www.businessinsider.com/5-of-albert-einsteins-thought-experiments-that-revolutionized-science-2016-7#imagine-youre-standing-in-a-box-4. And: https://news.nationalgeographic.com/2017/05/einstein-relativity-thought-experiment-train-lightning-genius/

6 Ibid. Also a good summary of the theory of relativity may be found at: https://www.space.com/17661-theory-general-relativity.html

7 D&C 9:7-10

8 D&C 88:118

9 https://blogs.scientificamerican.com/the-curious-wavefunction/leo-szilard-a-traffic-light-and-a-slice-of-nuclear-history/

10 http://www.storypick.com/inspirational-real-life-stories/

11 https://www.famousscientists.org/7-great-examples-of-scientific-discoveries-made-in-dreams/

12 Orson Pratt, *The Increased Powers and Faculties of the Mind in a Future State*, http://jod.mrm.org/2/235

Chapter 3 – Inspiration

▢ Image: David Porras/Shutterstock.com

1 http://www.glimling.com/blog/beethoven-was-right-about-walking/

2 https://www.psychologytoday.com/us/blog/habits-not-hacks/201407/beethovens-daily-habit-inspiring-creative-breakthroughs Also: At the University of Illinois Urbana-Champaign, functional MRI scans of walkers compared to a more sedentary control group established the link between walking and mental performance. After one year, people who took long walks showed a greater ability to detach from the outside world and more activity in the brain's network for complex tasks. https://news.illinois.edu/view/6367/205556

3 Moses 5:6

4 https://genius.com/John-cleese-lecture-on-creativity-annotated

5   Ibid.

6   https://www.beliefnet.com/columnists/bibleandculture/2009/12/
    handels-messiah-the-story-behind-the-classic.html

7   Neal A. Maxwell, *That Ye May Believe*, 183

8   Joseph B. Wirthlin, *Pondering Strengthens the Spiritual Life*,
    April 1982 General Conference

9   D&C 138:11

10 2 Nephi 4:15

11 3 Nephi 17:3

12 https://www.nytimes.com/2016/04/15/
    opinion/what-is-inspiration.html

13 https://www.fastcompany.com/3059634/
    your-brain-has-a-delete-button-heres-how-to-use-it

14 D&C 121:45

15 https://www.lds.org/general-conference/2012/04/how-to-obtain-
    revelation-and-inspiration-for-your-personal-life?lang=eng

16 Keith K. Hilbig, *Quench Not the Spirit Which Quickens
    the Inner Man*, October 2007 General Conference

Chapter 4 – Humor

□   Image: Ozgur Coskun/Shutterstock.com

1   James C. Humes, *The Wit & Wisdom of Benjamin Franklin*, 163

2   Matthew 23:24

3   http://kingsenglish.info/2011/10/07/
    strain-at-a-gnat-and-swallow-a-camel/

4   http://universe.byu.
    edu/2011/08/16/a-time-to-laugh-the-place-of-humor-in-the-church/

5   From an article written by his son Edward http://scholarsarchive.
    byu.edu/cgi/viewcontent.cgi?article=2389&context=byusq

6   http://www.azquotes.com/author/9852-David_O_McKay

7   Ibid, 24

8   Church News, September 1, 1995

9   https://msu.edu/~jdowell/morreall.html

10 Quoted in Walter F. Kolonosky, *Literary Insinuations:
    Sorting Out Sinyavsky's Irreverence*, 29

11 https://en.wikipedia.org/wiki/Russian_political_jokes

12 Viktor E. Frankl, *Man's Search for Meaning*, 54

Chapter 5 – Power

- Image: iStock.com/ThomasVogel
1 Moses 4:1
2 D&C 29:36
3 Moses 4:3
4 While there is no specific scripture so stating, it seems only logical that each spirit child of God, in realms created for eternal progress, would have to decide which path to take.
5 D&C 58:27-28
6 https://en.wikipedia.org/wiki/Maximilian_Kolbe
  And, yes, the man who cried out for his wife and children survived and lived until 1995.
7 "Priesthood Power," October 1999 General Conference
8 D&C 121:37
9 Mosiah 29: 13,16
10 D&C 101:77-80

Chapter 6 – Obey

- Image: Nejron Photo/Shutterstock.com
1 Matthew 8:27
2 A prominent example was around 74 B.C., Alma 44. Going back on an oath happened on occasion but so rarely that the word *repentance* was used to describe it, as per Mormon repenting of his oath not to lead Nephites into battle again (Mormon 5:1).
3 Alma 46:2
4 Alma 46:12
5 https://www.biblestudytools.com/dictionaries/eastons-bible-dictionary/covenant.html
6 Alma 46:21-24
7 Abraham 4:9-10, 12, 18; see also Helaman 12:7-17
8 Jacob 4:6
9 D&C 88:25-26
10 John A. Widtsoe, Rational Theology, 1915, 138
11 Abraham 4:12, Nibley's italics
12 https://scottwoodward.org/~scottwo2/Talks/html/z-Scholarly%20Articles/NibleyH_BeforeAdam.html
13 Abraham 3:22-23

14 D&C 130:19

15 Dallin H. Oaks, *Ensign*, Nov 1993, 72

16 Neal A. Maxwell, *Things as They Really Are*, 27, quoting *Journal of Discourses*. See also http://scottwoodward.org/ premortality_covenants.html 7:314-15

17 D&C 130:20-21

18 January 8, 2017, BYU

19 David A. Bednar, *Act in Doctrine* as quoted in https://ldsminds.com/obedience/

20 David A. Bednar, Rick's College devotional, September 9, 1997

21 D&C 84:38

Chapter 7 – Choose

▫ Image: Lightspring/Shutterstock.com

1 1 Corinthians 2:9

2 Alma 12:10-11

3 Neal A. Maxwell, *Grounded, Rooted, Established, and Settled*, BYU Devotional, September 15, 1981.

4 *Choices*, October 1990 General Conference

5 "Healing Your Damaged Life," *Ensign*, November 1992

6 2 Nephi 2:27

7 2 Nephi 2:29

Chapter 8 – Act

▫ Image: Krivosheev Vitaly/Shutterstock.com

1 2 Nephi 2:16

2 Alma 12:31

3 Mosiah 2:21

4 D&C 42:42

5 D&C 101:78

6 2 Nephi 2:16

7 D&C 29:39

8 2 Nephi 28:21

9 Tad R. Callister, *A Case for the Book of Mormon*, 201

10 https://en.wikipedia.org/wiki/Hurricane_Harvey

11 Washington Post, September 2, 2017

12 https://en.wikipedia.org/wiki/
    Gilbert_du_Motier,_Marquis_de_Lafayette

13 https://en.wikipedia.org/wiki/Leonardo_da_Vinci

14 https://en.wikipedia.org/wiki/Peter_the_Great

15 September 15, 2018

Chapter 9 – Opposition

▫ Image: iStock.com/FlyMint Agency

1 General Conference, Oct 2018

2 2 Nephi 2:11

3 2 Nephi 2:12

4 2 Nephi 2:13

5 http://villains.wikia.com/wiki/Nothing_(The_Neverending_Story)

6 2 Nephi 2:25

7 Dallin H. Oaks, *Opposition in All Things*,
    General Conference, April 2016

8 Matthew 18:7

9 Acts 14:22

10 Psalms 34:19

11 2 Nephi 20:10

12 D&C 98:3

13 2 Nephi 2:2

14 D&C 58:2-4

15 Quoted by Spencer W. Kimball in *Faith Precedes the Miracle*, 98

16 "Answers to Life's Questions," Ensign, May 1995

17 2 Corinthians 7:4

18 General Conference, October, 2017

19 Alma 7:11

20 John 16:33

Chapter 10 – Creativity

▫ Image: David Tadevosian/Shutterstock.com

1 https://caans-acaed.ca/Journal/issues_online/
    Issue_XVIII_2007/Kuretsky2007-1.pdf

2 Max Graf, *From Beethoven to Shostakovich – The
    Psychology of the Composing Process*, 1923, 92-96

- ☐ Image: Tithi Luadthong/Shutterstock.com
- 3 https://www.quotes.net/quote/68193

Chapter 11 – Innovation

- ☐ Image: Shaiith/Shutterstock.com
- 1 https://www.vox.com/2015/2/9/8004661/ fads-inventions-changed-world
- 2 https://science.howstuffworks.com/innovation/scientific-experiments/9-things-invented-or-discovered-by-accident7.htm
- 3 http://creativethinking.net/creative-thinking-technique-abstraction/#sthash.cLO4ClUH.dpbs
- 4 https://www.mnn.com/leaderboard/ stories/10-accidental-inventions-that-changed-the-world
- 5 https://www.sciencehistory.org/distillations/the-pursuit-of-sweet
- 6 https://interestingengineering.com/ james-watt-father-of-the-modern-steam-engine
- ☐ Image: Sergey Nivens/Shutterstock.com
- 7 Alexander Arbel, *Routes to the Information Revolution*, p 80-81 and https://en.wikipedia.org/wiki/Jacquard_loom

Chapter 12 – Prosperity

- ☐ Image: iStock.com/AlexRaths
- 1 https://www.carnegie.org/interactives/foundersstory/#!/
- 2 2 Nephi 1:20 and also 1 Nephi 2:20; 2 Nephi 4:4; Jarom 1:9; Alma 9:13; Alma 37:13
- 3 Mosiah 27:7
- 4 D&C 50:24
- 5 See for example: https://isi.org/ intercollegiate-review/10-prerequisites-for-prosperity/
- 6 Phil Gramm and Michael Solon, *Wall Street Journal*, April 20, 2017, A17
- 7 https://www.brainyquote.com/authors/milton-friedman-quotes
- 8 Data from the Federal Reserve Bank of Dallas
- 9 1 Nephi 22:23
- 10 2 Nephi 26:29
- 11 Helaman 7:21
- 12 Helaman 6:17

13 Helaman 6:8

14 2 Nephi 2:2

15 https://en.wikipedia.org/wiki/History_of_money#Banknotes_2

16 Moses 7:18

Chapter 13 – Objects

☐ Image: Sergey Nivens/Shutterstock.com

1 https://en.wikipedia.org/wiki/Otto_von_Bismarck

2 http://www.alexanderpalace.org/palace/rasputin-restaurant-joseph-vecchi.html

3 https://en.wikipedia.org/wiki/Grigori_Rasputin

☐ Image: Concept Photo/Shutterstock.com

4 1 Peter 4:15

5 3 Nephi 6:11

6 2 Nephi 1:18

7 https://thehill.com/policy/healthcare/247850-court-rules-nuns-group-must-comply-with-obamacare-birth-control-mandate

8 BYU Devotional, December 12, 2017

9 Neal A. Maxwell, *Things as They Really Are*, 34

10 David A. Bednar, *Seek Learning by Faith*, CES broadcast, February 3, 2006

11 James E. Faust, October 1995 General Conference.

12 1 John 3:8

13 D&C 121:41

14 Luke 17:3

15 Psalms 2:4

Chapter 14 – Intellectualism

☐ Image: Mike Baldwin/Cartoonstock.com

1 https://reason.com/2016/03/07/this-university-of-oregon-study-on-femin/

2 https://en.wikipedia.org/wiki/Anti-intellectualism

3 2 Nephi 9:28

4 Jeremiah 9:23

5 Romans 1:22

6 1 Cor. 3:19

7   Colossians 2:8

8   2 Timothy 3: 2, 7

9   2 Nephi 9:29

10   3 Nephi 6:12

11   Mosiah 29:26

12   Alma 51:8

13   Broadway play and movie *Camelot*.

14   http://www.pewresearch.org/fact-tank/2018/04/25/
     key-findings-about-americans-belief-in-god/

15   https://www.scientificamerican.com/article/
     is-social-science-politically-biased/

16   https://www.psychologytoday.com/us/blog/logical-take/201402/
     why-62-philosophers-are-atheists-part-i

17   https://afajournal.org/0907professors_religion.asp   Also:
     https://www.huffingtonpost.com/amarnath-amarasingam/
     how-religious-are-america_b_749630.html

18   https://news.stanford.edu/2017/02/21/the-threat-from-within/

19   Journal of Theoretical Humanities, Vol 20, 2015)

20   https://www.abc.net.au/religion/
     why-atheism-is-powerless-against-the-new-barbarians/10099800

21   https://www.researchgate.net/publication/256716854

22   Jacob 4:14

23   Mosiah 8:20

24   1 Nephi 12:18

25   2 Nephi 26:29

26   3 Nephi 6:15

27   Alma 1

28   2 Nephi 28: 4, 9

29   Luke 7:25

30   Mormon 8:28, 32-33, 36, 37

31   https://slate.com/news-and-politics/2018/05/televangelist-
     jesse-duplantis-asks-for-donations-for-private-jet.html

32   http://www.patheos.com/blogs/formerlyfundie/
     rich-pastors-peoples-stupidity/

33   Charles Dickens, *Dombey and Son*, 1848

34   1 Cor. 2:14

35   Dallin H. Oaks, *Witnesses of God*, BYU-Idaho, February 25, 2014

36 Oaks, ibid.

37 Wall Street Journal, 23 August 2013, A11

38 http://www.kairosjournal.org/document.aspx?DocumentID=6
     022&QuadrantID=3&CategoryID=6&TopicID=23&L=1

39 Isaiah 29:14

Chapter 15 – Distortion

▢ Image: Glenkar/Shutterstock.com

1 https://triblive.com/sports/
    biological-male-wins-ncaa-womens-track-championship/

2 http://mentalfloss.com/article/57032/25-words-are-their-own-opposites

3 Isaiah 5:20

4 Moroni 7:14

5 See Alma 11 for how the Nephites handled it.

6 Omni 1:17-18

7 Michael Michalko, "What I Learned About Creative Thinking
    from Aristotle" http://creativethinking.net/what-i-learned-
    about-creative-thinking-from-aristotle/#sthash.uaFPw0yf.dpbs

8 https://en.wikipedia.org/wiki/LGBT_history

9 Alma 30:18

10 Alma 1:20

11 October 2018 General Conference

12 https://blog.hubspot.com/marketing/gender-neutral-pronouns

13 https://www.nationalreview.com/2017/01/
    top-divinity-schools-use-gender-neutral-language-refer-god/

14 https://www.pewresearch.org/fact-tank/2017/11/08/
    transgender-issues-divide-republicans-and-democrats/

15 https://www.smithsonianmag.com/smart-news/
    there-are-37.2-trillion-cells-in-your-body-4941473/

16 Ignore Klinefelter's syndrome and Triple X syndrome;
    they still have male or female plumbing respectively.

17 Proclamation on the Family

18 Mosiah 29:27

19 Discourses of Brigham Young, 195

20 October 1999 General Conference

21 http://stevedunnhanson.com/tolerance-new-secular-morality/

22   Davies, Mark. (2007-) *TIME Magazine Corpus: 100 million words, 1920s-2000s.* Available online at https://www.english-corpora.org/time/

23   https://afajournal.org/past-issues/1994/march/word-abuse-a-political-lexicon/

24   https://www.npr.org/sections/memmos/2019/05/15/723678750/guidance-reminder-on-abortion-procedures-terminology-rights

25   BYU Devotional, October, 1978.

Chapter 16 – Centralization

▫   Image: iStock.com/CasPhotography

1   Stephen F. Hayward, "The Threat to Liberty" Claremont Review of Books, Winter 2016-17, 53-54.

2   https://teachingamericanhistory.org/library/document/leaders-of-men/

3   https://en.wikiquote.org/wiki/Milton_Friedman : *Capitalism and Freedom,* 1962

4   Temple Square Assembly Hall address, "Stand Up for Freedom" February 11, 1966.

5   Jacob 7:4

6   Alma 30:47

7   Alma 1:5

8   Mosiah 11:7

9   Alma 46:10

10   Mosiah 27:8

11   3 Nephi 3:2-10

12   2 Nephi 9: 42

13   See D&C 29

14   The Encyclopedia of Mormonism, http://eom.byu.edu/index.php/Stake

15   D&C 58:26

Chapter 17 – Statism

▫   Image: Epitavi/Shutterstock.com

1   https://www.freedomworks.org/content/19-ridiculous-federal-criminal-laws-and-regulations

2   https://www.rd.com/funny-stuff/dumbest-laws-america/?_cmp=readuprdus&_ebid=readuprdus7192019&_mid=291899&ehid=edb1a6aedc55856da731372fbd2b41bc64a0ad7

3 https://list25.com/25-stupid-government-regulations-that-will-make-you-shake-your-head/2/

4 *Democracy in America*, as quoted in http://www.truenorthquest.com/your-life-under-soft-despotism/

5 https://wagner.nyu.edu/files/news/Light-Op-Ed.pdf

6 http://www.centerforsmallgovernment.com/small-government-news/agencies-of-the-federal-government/

7 https://fas.org/sgp/crs/misc/R43590.pdf

8 https://regulatorystudies.columbian.gwu.edu/reg-stats

9 Ronald M. Hartwell in "The Politicization of Society," Wall Street Journal, August 21, 2013, A 11

□ Image: Pressmaster/Shutterstock.com

10 https://www.gregraven.website/real-motives/#more-2806

11 BYU Devotional, September 1981

12 Michael Goodwin, Imprimis, May-June 2017

13 http://www.powerlineblog.com/archives/2013/07/environmental-fraud-alert.php

14 Claremont Review of Books, Spring 2013, p 32.

15 https://en.wikiquote.org/wiki/Nancy_Pelosi Pelosi defenders claim the quote is out of context because she continued, "… away from the fog of controversy." But why should controversy require the bill be passed before we can see what is in it?

□ Image: Lightspring/Shutterstock.com

16 Federalist 62

17 Wall Street Journal, March 1, 2017, A18

18 Mark Chenoweth and Peggy Little, "Secret Laws for the Powerful," Wall Street Journal, July 24, 2019.

19 "The Tyranny of the Administrative State," Wall Street Journal, June 10, 2017

20 As quoted in Steven F. Hayward, *The Threat to Liberty*, Claremont Review of Books, Winter 2016-17, 54

21 Ronald Reagan's Farewell Address, January 11, 1989

22 *Wall Street Journal*, May 18, 1961

23 http://washingtonexaminer.com/mitch-mcconnell-slaps-irs-bonuses-says-public-sector-unions-bankrupting-country/article/2532230

24 Helaman 4:22; 5:2

25 http://www.mormonperspectives.com/?p=115

26 https://www.dennisprager.com/the-left-thinks-legally-the-right-thinks-morally/

27 Calvin Coolidge address on May 15, 1926, College of William & Mary.

28 https://www.foxnews.com/us/
    california-prop-47-shoplifting-theft-crime-statewide

Chapter 18 – Socialism

☐ Image: iStock.com/brackish_nz

1 Craig Biddle, *Individualism vs. Collectivism* in
   The Objective Standard, Spring, 2012

2 https://www.margaretthatcher.org/document/111266

3 http://freedomandprosperity.org/2015/blog/
   big-government/the-texas-grocery-store-that-helped-
   push-the-evil-empire-on-to-the-ash-heap-of-history/

4 Pew Research 2014

5 A favorite joke of Ronald Reagan

☐ Image: Pat Cross Cartoons

6 Jim Hunt, former governor of North Carolina at
   2012 Democratic National Convention

7 Alan Liotta, *Wall Street Journal*, August 25, 2017

8 *Economic Report of the President*, https://www.whitehouse.
   gov/wp-content/uploads/2019/03/ERP-2019.pdf

9 D&C 104:17

10 https://www.britannica.com/topic/vanguard-of-the-proletariat

11 Joseph Epstein, *Wall Street Journal*, May 30, 2019

12 Alma 42

13 Abraham 3:19

14 D&C 130:18-19

15 *Discourses of Brigham Young*, arranged by John A. Widtsoe, 318

16 *A Christmas Carol*, 11

17 http://www.epictimes.com/11/23/2014/
    thanksgiving-celebrating-the-birth-of-free-enterprise-in-america/

18 mises.org/library/thanksgiving-celebration-free-enterprise

19 https://www.2ndvote.com/
    panera-breads-socialism-experiment-in-ends-in-failure/

☐ Image: Leremy/Shutterstock.com

20 https://danieljmitchell.wordpress.com/2011/11/16/
    does-socialism-work-a-classroom-experiment/

21 Ludwig von Mises, *Socialism*, 1922

22 God's Prophets Speak, 324

23 https://en.wikipedia.org/wiki/John_William_Mackay

24 https://en.wikipedia.org/wiki/Crony_capitalism

25 https://en.wikipedia.org/wiki/Stakhanovite_movement

26 https://www.heritage.org/progressivism/commentary/
these-are-the-most-telling-failures-socialism

Chapter 19 – Tyranny

▫ Image: pixinoo/Shutterstock.com

1 https://en.wikipedia.org/wiki/Mass_surveillance_in_China

2 "Drones, facial recognition and a social credit system:
10 ways China watches its citizens," February 19, 2019

3 Celine Sui in *South China Morning Post*, August 5,2019

4 http://www.worldcoalition.org/China-reduces-the-number-of-crimes-
punishable-by-death-to-46-but-keep-drug-trafficking-in-the-list.html

5 https://en.wikipedia.org/wiki/Execution_van

6 BBC News, *Data leak reveals how China 'brainwashes'
Uighurs in prison camps*, November 24, 2019

7 Associated Press, June 3, 2019

8 Wall Street Journal, August 28, 2019, B3

9 Wall Street Journal, November 8, 2019, A15

10 *A Statement by President David O. McKay concerning the position of The
Church of Jesus Christ of Latter-day Saints on Communism*, July 1936

11 Wall Street Journal, *U.S. Companies Prop Up China's
Surveillance Network*, November 27, 2019, A1

12 Helaman 2:5

13 The Revolution Betrayed; What is the Soviet
Union and Where Is It Going?

14 https://www.bbc.com/news/world-asia-25363097

15 https://en.wikipedia.org/wiki/Great_Purge

16 https://en.wikipedia.org/wiki/Liu_Shaoqi

17 https://en.wikipedia.org/wiki/Jang_Song-thaek

18 Mormon 4:5

19 Alma 8:17

20 Ether 8:20

21 1 Nephi 14:3-4

22 Video, February 23, 2016 in Chile

Chapter 20 – Consequences

◻ Image: Naeblys/Shutterstock.com
1 https://en.wikipedia.org/wiki/Four_Pests_Campaign
2 D. Todd Christofferson, *Free Forever, to Act for Themselves*, October 2014 General Conference
3 Spencer W. Kimball, *Tragedy or Destiny*, BYU Devotional, December 1955
4 Alma 12:24
5 *The Righteous Judge*, October 2016 General Conference
6 https://www.smithsonianmag.com/innovation/if-necessity-mother-invention-then-play-its-father-180961107/
7 James E. Faust, *"Them That Honour Me I Will Honour"*, April 2001 General Conference
8 BYU Women's Conference, May 3, 2019
9 Thus, those who oppose abortion on demand must utilize more than monetary arguments.
10 Not that certain consequences can't be deflected. But such deflections are themselves actions for which another consequence stands ready. Sooner or later consequences catch up and the bill must be paid.
11 2 Nephi 28:8
12 Mormon 8:31
13 Alma 30:17
14 Alma 1:4
15 Helaman 13:27
16 October 2016 General Conference
17 An insightful discourse on this was given by Dr. Robert Matthews, former dean of Religious Education at BYU: *Why a Savior is Necessary, and Why Only Jesus Christ*, December 4, 1984: http://speeches.byu.edu/?act=viewitem&id=932

Chapter 21 – Victimhood

◻ Image: Zdorov Kirill Vladimirovich/Shutterstock.com
1 Alma 42:1
2 https://en.wikipedia.org/wiki/Victim_mentality
3 *Fiddler on the Roof*
4 Christian Schneider, Wall Street Journal, Aug 6 2019, A17
5 National Review November 27, 2017

6 Watterson, Bill. *Calvin & Hobbes.*

7 Alma 42

8 All atheists may not have a victim mentality, but those who do are more likely to be atheists than those who are Christians.

9 October 2016 General Conference

Chapter 22 – Responsibility

□ Image: pathdoc/Shutterstock.com

1 https://www.history.com/topics/9-11-attacks

2 https://www.psychologytoday.com/us/blog/inside-the-box/201401/creativity-lesson-betty-crocker

3 "The Desires of Our Hearts," Ensign, June 1986

4 D&C 101:78

5 Mormon 3:20

6 D&C 72:3

7 D&C 42:32

8 Mosiah 29:38

9 https://www.sperrybaseballlife.com/stay-at-17-inches/

10 *Teachings of the Presidents Of the Church: Wilford Woodruff,* 205

Chapter 23 – Experience

□ Image: Mark Carrel/Shutterstock.com

1 Journal of Discourses 1:148

2 https://en.wikipedia.org/wiki/Chesley_Sullenberger

3 D&C 122:7

4 https://en.wikipedia.org/wiki/Military_career_of_George_Washington

5 Luke 22:61-62

6 Romans 5:3-4

7 Romans 12:12

8 Acts 26:20

9 Helaman 4:15

10 Romans 12:2

□ Image: iStock.com/HughStoneIan

11 *Truth and the Plan,* General Conference, October 2018

Chapter 24 – Exaltation

- ▫ Image: Romolo Tavani/Shutterstock.com
- ▫ Image: Travel Stock/Shutterstock.com

1 https://www.churchofjesuschrist.org/study/manual/gospel-principles/chapter-47-exaltation?lang=eng

2 D&C 76:69,62

3 Lorenzo Snow

4 D&C 132:19-20

5 *Discourses of Brigham Young*, 57

6 Quoted in chapter 47 in the Gospel Principles manual.

7 Moses 1:33-38

8 1 Corinthians 2:9

9 D&C 14:7